m-Talá

CHUS PATO

m-Talá

translated by Erin Moure

Shearsman Books & BuschekBooks
Exeter   Ottawa

First published in the United Kingdom in 2009 by
Shearsman Books Ltd
58 Velwell Road
Exeter EX4 4LD   www.shearsman.com

ISBN 978-1-84861-045-3

and in Canada by
BuschekBooks
P O Box 74053
Ottawa, Ontario K1M 2H9   www.buschekbooks.com

ISBN 978-1-894543-54-5

Acknowledgements
An excerpt from this translation, entitled *from m-Talá,* was published by
Nomados (Vancouver, Canada) in 2003.
Cover image: code of Hammurabi, photograph copyright © John Said, 2007.

Library and Archives Canada Cataloguing in Publication

Pato, Chus, 1955-
    m-Talá / Chus Pato ; translated by Erín Moure.

Translation of the Galician book by the same title.
Poems.
Co-published by: Shearsman Books.
ISBN 978-1-894543-54-5

    I. Mouré, Erin, 1955- II. Title.

PQ9469.2.P37M7313 2009   869.15   C2009-901389-4

Contents

Translating Chus Pato

The first time I read publicly from my translation of *m-Talá*, I sent Chus Pato a photo of the event, and she emailed me back from Lalín where she lives in Galicia, in the very northwest of Spain, to say she felt welcomed into English-language poetry.

I think that this is part of what having a literature is: to invite others to join it, to exist in its language, not as foreign but as different, as glad bearers of a difference which strengthens, in the paradoxical way that difference does have of bringing strength. To me, part of nurturing poetry in a national literature is welcoming a voice from another language into our own, and letting it change our own language.

To invite a work across a border is to open the self to something new, for translation upsets and opens a reader's own habits in their native (or other!) tongue. Chus Pato has upset mine, and in ways neither she or I could predict. Sometimes such openings also open the language, open English, in this case.

The prime example of this process, of course, in our tongue, is Henry Howard, Earl of Surrey, and his 16th century translation of books 2 and 4 of Virgil's *Aeneid*. Howard responded to the demands of the Latin original by creating a new form in English. and though his publisher called the result "this strange meter," blank verse has since been inextricably associated with our poetry.

No wonder, then, that translation beckons glad foment into my own writing practice, and its effect reverberates in my own poetry, and through that poetry, into the poetry of others. Translation expands the range of what is possible, and in unpredictable ways!

Chus Pato is a poet whose work through the 1990s, culminating in *m-Talá* at the turn of the century, has had a phenomenal effect in Galician literary culture. As María do Cebreiro, herself a fine poet in Galician, once said, upending Pato's own words: *m-Talá* is a poker game of impurities—and writing about it is like sending a postcard home from a foreign country: there's so little space, so much to say.

Chus Pato was born María Xesús Pato (Chus is a diminutive of María Xesús) in Ourense, in the interior of Galicia—a green equivalent, oh, of Osoyoos, BC if Osoyoos had been founded by the Romans who had left a bridge in a valley topped by hills that had previously harboured Celtic towns. Pato was born in 1955, the year I too was born, but I was born in Calgary in Canada, and Pato in a region of the state of Spain that is not Spanish. She grew up speaking Galician—that language of a 1,300-year-old kingdom joined to Spain in a monarchical shuffle 900 years ago, and language at the root of modern Portuguese. Yet Galicians, ordinary Galicians, have maintained their difference, their Galician language and culture. Despite the odds.

Pato and I may have similar wary, hopeful, discordant poetic sensibilities but our background and work have differences, too. Fundamental ones that extend to the way we each grew up. The country into which Chus was born was ruled by a fascist dictatorship, that of Franco, which endured until she was 20. In her childhood, the pain of the era called *posguerra* still lingered strongly in the silences and divisions, in the poverty and hunger of a people overshadowed by the pomp of state and church. In one poem she wrote: "My native language is fascism." It's a statement that slaps, defiant but sad too. While acknowledging her education and the tenor of her native land and upbringing, she goes on to defy it, by writing in Galician—a language oppressed under Franco, not taught in schools, not published except very marginally and late and in allegory, or by exiles in Argentina—and of a republic that is yet to come. Pato is not interested in essentializing ethnicity, but she wants to speak her own language, in a place where it's not always—even today—easy to do so. Language itself propels her for another reason: *it's a freedom-machine*. It breaks with every code. It opens possibles that no other regime can.

The year Pato was 20, in 1975, Franco died, or they pulled the plug on him, and in 1976 Spain could finally open doors to Europe. Some of my Spanish friends who grew up in that era grew not even knowing that the government overthrown in a coup on July 18, 1936 by General Francisco Franco had been democratically elected. They learned that and many things after

1976, and quickly. People emerged from shadow into official culture, more or less. It was a time of conflicting codes, codes newly legal, speech newly legal amid the death rattle of old fears, words newly minted that could be seen—when the carnival slowed down—as part of a culture that was larger and more multiple than central Spain would admit to. And this still holds true today. The smaller, "peripheral" nationalities in the Spanish state have not yet received their due. For many reasons. Part of it was a successful "transition to democracy" that involved a "national reconciliation" which let the same people step into democratic power without answering for past collusion with repression, a transition thus partly built (and still is—though slowly it changes) on a silence that to many seemed necessary at the time. One result is that old cadavers, bones, crushed skulls, bits of cloth and coat-buttons, still lie covered in ditches in Galicia and elsewhere. There's a restlessness not just in Galicia, but in Spain, that keeps surfacing, for memory doesn't go away that easily, even with the shiny surfaces of capitalist economy as distraction. It's readily acknowledged that the American Civil War still affects America; the Spanish Civil War, much more recent, can't help but have its reverberations in today's Spain.

1976 also happily and powerfully marked other trajectories, such as that of poetry in Galician. That year, *Con pólvora e magnolias—With Gunpowder and Magnolias*—was published by Xosé Luís Méndez Ferrín, a writer of intensely beautiful and galvanizing prose, poetry, essays and journalism who would be world-famed if he wrote in the idiom of the central state, but he chose Galician. This book marked a radical change in the course of poetry in Galicia, in its "modernization", in its political commitment and its resonant and powerful use of the language, in its wide and sure step away from feeding the myth of a purely rural, docile culture that can't raise its voice, that is not "educated" unless it writes in Spanish.

Chus Pato's *m-Talá* marked, in 2000, a further rupture, an invitation across a boundary. It is considered a turning point in Galician poetry. Its strange title is a word with no meaning in Galician; it's untranslatable. People have said *m-Talá* is an unpronounceable, untranslatable cry. Yet, unbeknownst even to Pato, perhaps, it echoes pertinent realities. In the Temi language of Tanzania, "mtala" means "sudden apparition." In the American tongue, EMTALA is a law to stop hospitals from dumping desperately ill patients who are uninsured, unable to pay. Pato's *m-Talá* is her own sudden apparition into discourses that harm us, in searing poetry that identifies the sickness, refuses no treatment, and—without being a hospital—sends no one away. For me, it's a name that seems to have risen from the cradle of written western culture. Yet Chus Pato's work faces not the past, but the future, and our future selves.

In *m-Talá*, Pato refuses to maintain the illusion that the lyric "I" is the personal voice of the poet. She refuses the singularity of poetic voice altogether, taking on voices till she *is* these voices, these pantonymic heteronyms, this chorus in which Agape, cyborgs, Raida's astral body and Brenda jostle alongside Mephisto, Kafka, Poe, Ferrín, Celan, Lautréamont, and Rimbaud. Here every doorway *is* rainbow and fruit, wave and dérive. *m-Talá* is a wild and assured romp through histories that are literary and geographical, geopolitical and local, gendered and national. As Pato has said, she writes "after the deluge" where "the void is not a limit, it's a passage."

In Pato's hands, Galician is dynamic, radicalized language. The language of a woman alive in history who names a country. A language droll and fierce, which is to say, one of optimism. Or hilarity. She plays with every code imaginable: gender coding, positioning of the spectator, positioning of the poet, the identity of the author, in ways that we are more used to seeing in theatre or visual art. Or in Fernando Pessoa, perhaps. She uses radio interview, dramatic dialogue, letters, diaries, ticket stubs, screams. She is Chus, Brenda, Nefertiti, and the writer in her study in Galicia weighing potatoes at her desk. Her work is flow and clamour, snicker and oration, bellow and murmur, outcry and dance, and it stops for breakfast at 6 a.m. in a deserted railway station in Monforte and gives up literature altogether.

Only to take it up again. And we readers are glad she does.

Erín Moure
Fredericton, Montreal

our history: *incised into*
granite from which dreams are made

belén feliú

i ask myself if in this phrase all the yews of the free city
of Paris lean and fall, all my reflections on language—the word
that shuts the edifice of Language is the same that opens to the
wind's dominion—it was possible in those days to cross not just
one but two, three, endless rainbows, each portal and fruition;
to you, I wanted to say "onyx," to tell you Camille sculpted "the
wave" and three figurines of bronze, and who can say if the
waters are fertility, flow. I dreamed of the sewers, of the king's
libido or rather his absence of libido, out by the pond, pondering
the total dearth of desire in an art devoid of passion with only
calculation and the aesthetics of calculation to trace the guiding
principles of its trade. The waters: what an architecture to
house civilizations, sister! Babel is time and Aphrodite. I craved a
Ganges of words; how terrible these tresses are, whose sole clasp
is my hand and sole emblem, the wind! It's like waking from a
dream, of the body, of words

the lake

we're lost, we turn in circles to get out
they traverse the huts
hers, her memories, sad, amiable and sad—target
for gunshot at the fringes of whatever city. *He* utters sentences,
I don't know if I'm to transcribe the sentences *He* utters or not,
they're phrases about the baffling semiotic of signs.
She launches into her story: about minks, knows mink farms
have always existed, knows they'll bite the swan's neck, in the
artery, the congealed blood is sperm on any altar, cetaceous.
You utter the most beautiful phrase of all
—Sirius is blue

to be inscribed on the skins of 101 dalmations, in the
slaughterhouses of Chicago, Cincinnati, Chicago.

Or the book's engravings would sear my eyes

PS: it's all about liquefaction of blood; they'd always used sperm,
dyed: above 10°C it no longer coagulates so when the believers
cram into the temple, the prodigy spontaneously occurs. In the
text, it means She could have felt like that, object of superstition
and veneration, and it could also be a metaphor for the poem,
pouring out over all past liturgies. As for those slaughterhouses,
my love for the study of contemporary history will absolve this
thought that masks such dark dissolution, Lautréamont Terrace
—the huge pedestals eroded, the colossal fractures. The dawn,
of course, is the dawn of Patroclus.

(with Xosé Luís Méndez Ferrín)

leaning on a tree, not breathing. Have to solve this problem,
I don't accept the non-dissolution, mystic or otherwise, of a
body into any Mother Nature. Next, the video scenes: abducted,
reverberations in the capsule, I feel the reverberations bend
me double, will you unbend me, in the marrow, shelter me
there, you on the verge of turning into Jupiter, and me into
Danae—what's left of you a flower, the wettest flower in your
hair—guarding flocks.
Quartz of words
cuneiform
from the inside
i'm translucent.
Filiform, of words

you can't see the battle because it's far off, in Eritrea
the painting's monstrous, three or four times bigger than an
opera backdrop. The mother, one of the lad's four mothers, will
speak and does. Nothing; in some symbolic place the mushroom
turns into a maiden
—just look at her little hood and lepiota cloak
intuit her body, svelte and tigery, her touch, cold. How icy it
is among the mushrooms when night falls. Surprised and glad
because you can pull your hand away and glove your fingers or
warm them in your pockets. She's mute, naturally. There's only
the perfect name of God, the name of Antonin Artaud where
someone bares the stone. Great sheets of rain into it, miles
down, deep with damp dead leaves and since you're late you
crouch in chestnut husks where children sleep with solar tiaras
and rock themselves and one of the four mothers will speak and
does in this bedroom dedicated to Sterne because that's where
we are, in the grimorium of a poet, and Julia Moesa tells how
she had to wade through twenty-five yards of manure to find a
lost bit off the milking machine,
and everyone gazes, miles down, the pages of the Outre-tombe
frozen to kill bookworms, to cure it of evil, and they all breathe
and the stone must be cloaked again

what we'll never figure out is if we're inside or not, if the
teardrop is jet or basalt, if inside are the three dancing witches, if
we'll someday tunnel to the open. The stone compacts itself, as
in a zigguri ritual. Just notice the initials, white and red initials,
of the royal male-sun, and the female-sun, royal. We'll never find
out if our nerves are solar emanations, if the page is parasitical
on the secretions of my brain
our nerves radiant with saffron in the letters of the betyl
Especially when the losses are so violent and close

Veracruz, May 1947.

i've reached a place where pain impedes thought, my brain
works like an image-factory—or more exactly, a sea of hearts. So
right now they're distending, morphing into flat surfaces, filling
sea to the horizon. They suggest huge leaves of tropical plants,
carnivorous, then strewn islands, Saint Brendan's, verdant, all
these sands flowering in the sea
—look for me in the direction of the Indies
huge scarlet bubbles, floating in the shipwreck—then aprons are
pin-ups, they invade the waters as far as the eyes can see

      keep faith
      never write these words down

      idols of the heart

Forty years staring at the wall, windowed, on the same grand
scale as the Carthage airport
so the air can split in two

and crown itself

that's it, they killed me, or how the poet abandons the
rites of autumn to become human

the queen had a heart
—yummm, so tasty!

silently
like Krishnamurti
silently

because all of it was already too screwed up to have to deal with
that if democracy and yes, we all ended up on i don't know what
kind of shitty union epiphany-list, it was sort of like hearing
talk of doors
—get out!

then nothing
not a single, single, death

                                                        left

my heart's rhythm is so fast astral, I'd be better off tending
geraniums, martian-aliens,
—okay, come in
touch them, they line the cell, Pausilipos-uterus, golden, like
fleece.
Here you'll hear talk, all that stuff on the reproductive capacity
of the female of the biological and not so biological species,
model for so many other forms
—got it straight? because you'd better get it; that is, NO
MOTHER-NATURE
waits for us. Not even when we're dead, none of us will
ever again be able to dissolve in any MOTHER-nature. ETHER.
Except some of us (retrograde)
AS METAPHORS
ETERNALLY
AGRARIAN

      you select the saddest path
      a verdant landscape: glacée
      that's how autumns come to an end

because we leap without a net, to do it we take "abyss lessons"
I'd better be nice
find things to do that make me smile
That's how we survive:
me and you too, my favourite alien
outside the womb

just like huge Polar Bears on the ice-floes of Greenland

i, Davinia Bardelas saw, on that day of December 18th,
saw it all. Saw the SLAUGHTER. Saw how from the sow's neck,
immemorial, gushed litres of blue-blood and it all unfolded as if
on the boards of a medieval banquet;
how a man in blue overalls was spattered by the filthy spray
in the agony of the death-rattle and how two troughs were readied
under parallel branches, like railroad tracks
that won't meet and finally flare up

They're the two great emblems of December

      and this one you're going to read, the infinite of Language

eternity is me, in the middle of the study, weighing on an invisible
scale an entire harvest of potatoes

      la mer allée / avec le soleil

and that's how autumns really come to an end.

—God help us, Gordon!, whose grimy blazer are you
wearing?
—I think you're mistaken, sir, my name's not Gordon or Gordin
and really you should take note of my new blazer and
don't go on saying grimy blazer

from sky to sea, in blues. All bathed in this light: dusk.
Akhmatova walks out of the market. It's the woman whom
Nathan I. Altman once painted
—later I'll take on the look of a poisoned woman, dead
her belly bloated
and a scarlet stain across one eye
In this light, Gordon enters, his movements torpid, slow, a sailor-
jacket over his first disguise

    (the ballet: a polyphony; and in the polyphony: Arthur
Gordon Pym's granddad; Gordon Pym; Quirón, Atlantic
centaur; Akhmatova; Mnemosyne of graceful figure adorned
with vast muslin shawl and flounces, face heavily made-up; City
with matronly bearing; Arthur Rimbaud, radiant Orpheus; Xosé
Luís Méndez Ferrín and Paul Celan, poets; Narrator-hostess; and
Ezra, poet) / / it's up to the reader to match characters to voices;
the author claims she knows perfectly who's who but it's not
always obvious.

----

hey Arthur! without a last name, country, god. Arthur shoots
dice with fate

—disguises, because for Arthur Gordon Pym the imagination is
the sole experience, of the real, of life

—the south's fanged scarlet? Ethiopian root? will the south be a
towering giantess? or white spume, where the abyss opened?

The abyss was triple: the Yeni Gui, the Grampus and the canoe;
will the south be manna? white mist, vapour or ash?

—I'd scarcely descended when I started to dress up like Rogers'
corpse, my shirt the kind of blue fabric blouse white-striped that
the dead man wore over other clothing—.
That done, I faked a belly using blankets; the effect was perfect,
they said I was Rogers from top to toe. Peters smeared my face
with chalk then with blood he squeezed from a cut finger: "a
huge carmine stain across the eye." For sure, my presence was
repugnant
—red eyes, blood-injected: elixir, life
—the voyage is Ocean, a mystical geometry that made the
young Gordon a disciple of the Orpheans and Pythagoreans

—will we gloss over the racism of Arthur Gordon Pym, will we
even dare to mention Edgar?
—native women have black teeth?

—it's total insensitivity to think native women's teeth are black
—the helmsman is tipsy
—there might have been twenty-five or thirty, scattered from
stern to the galleys. It was clear that there was no living soul
aboard that ship, disaster
—we spotted a figure very tall and strong, still bent over the
gunwales, head ever swaying, his face turned so we couldn't see
it. At his waist where his shirt was pulled out, the petrel landed;
it avidly ate the telefax, its plumage bloody.

Arthur picks up its heart
—after we exhaust once and for all some parts of the romantic
lexicon we hit upon three or four paragraphs of singular beauty.
BALTHAZAR'S FEAST (Rembrandt): hologram
—could Arthur have gone up and grabbed control of the boat?

An apparent boat, but Arthur is *un autre* just as Akhmatova is *une autre*

—"I've seen things you people wouldn't believe. Attack ships on fire off the shoulder of Orion. I watched C-beams glitter in the dark near the Tannhäuser gate. All those moments will be lost in time, like tears in rain"

—now there's gooseneck barnacles, sharks, port wine: here's to crustaceans, to the salt bath of the Caribbean!

—we know Arthur never left his room, never saw the sea, would never embark on it

—dregs all over my face, and great blocks of granite. Babylon destroyed

—if only the schooner weren't so sturdy, if the captain had lacked zeal, if it weren't well-equipped
—it should have, for sure, ten or twelve small 12-calibre guns and two or three larger

—our heads above water barely one second out of three

—third speculative ending: when we rose from the cave we reached the platform, a patch of blue: conflagration
—soon catching rigging, masts, the ruin of the sails, the fire tore across the deck
—the labyrinth, curse of literature
—free / a path through human- / shaped snow (Celan)
—birds, the white *corina*. We leapt into the waterfall

—i carved it on the mountain, in the mist of the cliff. The chronicle of this woeful CATASTROPHE
—i confess my love for your late wife
—huh . . . late wife? who? reading your poems, it's impossible to tell middle from beginning or end, will you speak clearly for

once if you want me to listen
—ROOKERY's a pretty name for an orphanage
—now what's a rookery?

Enter Sylvia Plath, very young, very beautiful, blond and tanned.
As in the photos of her Costa Brava honeymoon. Enter three
radiant orphans—the page bathed in gold—they climb on what's
left of the Grampus
—Akhmatova arise! we'll head to the city of the seven daggers
—I don't want to run into the one who used to sport an agate
necklace
Heading straight for a lineage, without destiny

AND ONE YEAR LATER
pallid in the wine-red algae. Eleutheria, gorgeous Daphne in
ocean sands

I am nectar
ambrosia

—BECAUSE IT'S NOT ONLY LANGUAGE THAT'S
UNDER THREAT BUT OUR VERY LINGUISTIC CAPACITY,
regardless of the idiom we speak

LANGUAGE IS PRODUCTION, language produces, produces
COMMUNICATION, PRODUCES THOUGHT, PRODUCES
POETIC CAPACITY,
produces profit and gain, PRODUCES US as HUMANS,
produces us as HAPPINESS

Language is PRODUCTION, thus CAPITAL's attempts to
PRIVATIZE language, to leave us WORDLESS

LANGUAGE, any LANGUAGE UNDER CAPITAL, tends
to wither, to be converted into an object to consume. Into
something we as speakers no longer PRODUCE, but which
CAPITAL, in its attempt to privatize us, PRODUCES FOR US

Under CAPITAL the creators of Language, its speakers, turn
into

CONSUMERS; Language, any Language under Capital,
becomes a consumer product, the same as any other
MERCHANDISE

LANGUAGE-LINGUISTIC SERVITUDE
KAPITAL-KILLER
ASSASSIN

                              (with Paco Sampedro)

—there's eight boats in a row
—twenty-four
—twenty-seven, sir
when the fog lifted we knew the enemy's strength. We advanced
pell-mell like squadrons that break rank and leap singly into the
fray. They'd cut the cables. I remember ships breaking for open
sea and the bowsprit—waves towering!—argh the waves lashed
us. So that we dived into the thick of it, twenty-four boats and
the rear-guard totally surrounded
—if we keep on, sir, we'll run aground: Arousa and arousal—
—I don't care if there's fifty of them, attack!
our boats are hearts of oak, our brigantines twins of shining
copper
"o'er the sea into my bower/ comes he who bears love's flower"
Onega remembered ships and the boy's arm and torchlight
dancing across the deck, the story of Jeanne de Belleville
—traitor, him? traitor? Philip de Valois was the real traitor, he
launched his most powerful armed galleys then got lost, without
victuals or water, between strange reefs and islands, Oliverio de
Clisson's son dying in that mother's arms, lady of Fortune
From prow to poop, flames leapt, beneath what one witness
called "moonlight's cold pallor." Masts collapsed in the sea's
phosphorus, in the heart of the battle, Eleanor, Elenship,
Eletpolis, Eleanor, destroyer of ships, of cities, Eleeeeeeanor!!!,
blood through the portholes, on the diamond, the hoist. We fell
between puffs of artillery smoke, one by one, the beer soured
and bread good only for casting overboard
—cut the line, sir
Sacau burst in with all the ships of the Corme division
—have you seen sea-swallows on September dunes? such were
Sacau's resisting forces. The Nebrija destroyed

At daybreak the Admiral Kumiko Heathrow swept out his own
quarters and fed the chickens

horseshoes in the cliffs and clefts, the Jamaican ensign in the depths
—get back to your post if you don't want to be summarily shot
drowning in your own tears
in the sea's woes
in yours
Eros.

what the author can't stand, what she's not about
to put up with, is the disappearance of Cordelia Manannan
MacLear, so she invents this scene: the Impossible Resurrection
of Cordelia's dead body; whether the poem really exists or not
hardly matters, or whether it's just the seed of a disappearance;
the poet will check each vessel all over again, each of the heroes
THEY DON'T EXIST

"of the strange wheezes of her brother whom they wake up
with the ballads of Otis Redding
over me, too, who absorbs with delight the empire of the death
of the father who could not be *initiator into the game*"
—just take a look and step back now, breathe, and keep your
distance:

the curtain rises:

GD.#1: China was immense, just ask me, I'm a Chinese woman.
We'll spend our honeymoon there, swim, we'll be so happy
GD.#2: we'll talk of trees, where Flint rests in the foundations.
I had another lover, a mathematician, he told me about Cantor,
about the infinite, the theories of Cantor
GD.#1: here we are in the woods, gravedigger # 1 and
gravedigger #2, or just plain #1 and #2
#2: Cordelia speaks, as if by instinct, addressing certain thoughts
to her father
CORDELIA: I just want to say I'm not sure it's worth all that
insistence on "transport." Metaphor invariably leads to a world
of static essences. But you, my lord, are mute as sun in my
sphere's core. We'll see if grammars don't think, if no thought
stems from grammar. You'll all die later, after five long acts, each
one more apocalyptic; such agony was the time of my youth.
Nonetheless I never had any problem with all of you, and my
death in an earlier episode broke your heart, that heart I couldn't

bring to my lips: my dear father, my madman!

GD#1: all listen! do you hear the sea?

CORDELIA: I will bury my mother, dead and well buried, but in dreams: black and perfect Shade, her jealousy, that I'm not her. She sings and every nation. Awakens.

you're not my mother! and you could never be my mother, even dead

—MOTHER.

And so she still loved this miserable spot

these ruined walls

(in the background, blurred, Joseph, Mary and the ectoplasm baby walk. Headed toward Egypt)

from here onward, the gravediggers are called #1 and #2

#2: on a tree branch?

#1: yes, by a river, she was braiding a garland of flowers, she was someone, almost a non-someone, she travelled tucked in a star, she said

#2: we're building gallows! but not near the latrines. She lay with Yahweh, with her five hundred fathers who never engendered her

#1: will mandrakes take root in her? "I shall not eat nor drink until the Lord my God cometh unto me," and so I pitch my tent

#2: it's a love story?

#1: yes, a great story, but today I'm not picking up the plates

#2: I'm not scrubbing the kitchen

#1: I'm not picking up the plates

#2: I'm not going to the pool

#1: I'm not picking up the teapot

#2: out of the fog, every morning, a huge Moebius strip

#1: or in the metro, they flash their raincoats and ta-da, you learn about the dicky-bird!

#2: glad is the path and glad those who walk upon it

#1: we'll have a hot time! corpses at the scaffold, I must confess, were the style back then

#2: don't say I didn't warn you

#1: putrid, dead, destroyed, I'm always stumbling upon them

#2: words

#1: no, I mean Dracula

Dracula wins by a hair, for he's got his own barber and even
at the most hopeless moments he's coiffed with consummate
perfection and art and so he wins
he always beats
Yahweh
#2: many sleep eternally on the shelves
#1: you'll just waste your pencils
#2: a cozy spot to spend the summer
#1: a winter poem
#2: the infinite web of my anxiety
DETECTIVE #1: I have to take stock of things. Where do I stand?
The author is terrorized, it terrorizes her that her body or any
other body can't dissolve in any Mother-Nature and that only
air envelops it. That's why she decided to build a quartz, a coffin
where she'd bury lilacs, which somehow would be milky or
clear. She decided too to write down all those absurd dialogues
in the forest, dialogues of love, of love's stupidity, its babble,
of the tenderness of this love. On top of that, there's Shkspr
and her readings of the canon, the whole question of literary
jealousy and anxiety of influence, and above all this obsession
with Lear and especially with Cordelia; what does she see, what
on earth does she see that so impressed her in Lear?
firstly the tempest, then later, the tempest and Cordelia
the author's trying to make us believe in Cordelia's Resurrection,
she'd like to believe in it herself, so it must be *her* who crosses
the stage with the dead body of her friend or even she herself
mixed in with Cordelia crosses the stage in the arms of her
father Lear-Moses-Yahweh-Dracula, not to mention Sade,
another of her imaginary fathers but, how to dethrone Lear?
Cordelia just sleeps, the author wants to believe this, believe
that this simulated disappearance'd provoke a torpor in Lear
who'd immediately recognize in the sleeping one a filiation
infinite and without destiny, then abdicate in terror. And then
there are all these ectoplasmic bodies that intrigue her and this
fantasy in which Cordelia makes love with 500 fathers who never
engendered her, Cordelia lies with her 500 fathers coalesced in
one big Yahweh-Dracula memory.

This is the real scene of the Impossible Resurrection of Cordelia
Manannan MacLear, daughter of the sea, or Lucia, Anna, Cordelia,
Livia—as she's known in other manuscripts.
In the intestines, in the burbling guts of God, our heroine,
according to what the author wants to believe, could finally read
her own design, her own stone tablets.
The author fails, of course
#1: didn't I tell you you should bring your pencil and paper,
later you won't remember a thing
#2: is it finished?
#1: we'll never know anything of Cordelia, or of what she intends
#2: is the author Cordelia?
#1: you're so out of it; the author is a lady married to a gentleman
#2: so it's true!
#1: only a virtuous body like Justine's could stand such a slow, long
siege
#2: but it can't be easy to nab a father
#1: she's resolute, keeps trying, later too there's all her work with
the mothers, the all-powerful mothers, and you know what she
does, she buries them, but they revive, right when she gets them
underground, right when she's got them tamped down, and they
resuscitate, alive of course
#2: that's how she gains a knowledge, an intimate knowledge of
the father, in her own flesh, the author wants to make us believe
that Cordelia is the poem and that the poem requires murder to be
able to tell its story in the poem, to make us believe that Cordelia is
queen of the antigrammatical cyborgs that think themselves up in
language, and thus language is what's closest to "Nature"
Ectoplasm of baby Jesus: on earth I'm fatherless and I'm motherless
in heaven, I'll explain it to you all again, good soldier, though I
realize you understand nothing; see these clay pigeons? okay then
watch, I'll just blow on them and there you are, the pigeons fly
#1: my head hurts, my head's killing me
#2: we could go on a trip, plan to sail forth for the first time
#1: but I have to monitor in the library, it's not on my schedule but
it's written on every wall
#2: you're gorgeous, woman

#1: my trousers don't match my sweater
#1: are we off?
#2: to where?
#1: we could visit Homunculus in the Sea of Galilee
#2: but Homunculus died, died from otherness, from love
#1: okay then, to Egypt
#2: to Cairo
#1: what's in Cairo?
#2: I don't know, I hear there's . . . gnomes
#1: yes, the emperor of gnomes, Peer Gynt by name, is in a
Cairo madhouse
#2: I hope when the treatment's finished, my head stops hurting
#1: you liked it?
#2: yes, because it's a love story, I almost sobbed from all the
tenderness at the end, it's a story in which love, the grandson of
spume, can survive anything
#1: a tomb
#2: a mausoleum
#1: for whom?
#2: for her, my beloved

curtain

(*Discovery Enterprise:* Nation of Stars or
Lasciate ogni speranza -------- possible title for this short play or
little theatre)

the author builds a forest with each stick, each fable; the forest is
the legacy of her dead friend Cordelia M. Mac Lir
post-tempest, post-night of the storm that Love honours in the
poem.
The short play or fantasy unfolds in this very forest
in 24 cantos 24 puffs of gunpowder
whose vertices are snowy

UNPOETICIZABLE
previously impossible
like robots, without blood-ties

but not fake either
THEY FOUND

the trammeled tongue (ouch) of kid goats

MEPHISTO: so, madame, that's what you think was the cause of death?

AGAPE: yes, that's what I think

MEPHISTO: and when did you start to suspect?

AGAPE: upon her return

MEPHISTO: but how do you explain it? wasn't she travelling for pleasure?

AGAPE: yes but there were also family reasons. Nonetheless it couldn't have happened in the north, where Dora had visited her family, but in the south, once she'd left for the south

MEPHISTO: did she mention waterfalls?

AGAPE: she spoke of a veil over a promontory and the happy roar of water

MEPHISTO: happy?

AGAPE: she had an endless capacity, even brought maple syrup and discussed the differences between types of syrup

MEPHISTO: how to explain, then, the sudden change?

AGAPE: I can't figure it out myself, there must be another reason

MEPHISTO: America?

AGAPE: yes, America

MEPHISTO: I think I recall that many Eastern Europeans put their hopes on America

AGAPE: it's the story of the "stoker," that first chapter of Kafka. The disappearance, the strange disappearance of Dora Diamant

MEPHISTO: you insist on using that word

AGAPE: I never saw her body, and wasn't at the burial

MEPHISTO: but there's medical proof

AGAPE: naturally, there's that certificate, we even know she arranged to donate all her organs and that they were extracted from her

MEPHISTO: and then?

AGAPE: I might as well talk of enigmas

MEPHISTO: I don't follow you, I can't understand you, madame
AGAPE: we can hardly put it into words
MEPHISTO: but there's an explanation
AGAPE: yes, a "reasonable" explanation
MEPHISTO: when she came back?
AGAPE: the moment she returned, at that exact instant
MEPHISTO: and you didn't ask her?
AGAPE: I tried to broach the subject
MEPHISTO: did she listen to you?
AGAPE: it was impossible, despite her willingness, she was
exquisite, then of course the hospitalizations started
MEPHISTO: the pain was clearly diagnosed?
AGAPE: yes
MEPHISTO: and Dora, did she say anything about it?
AGAPE: by letter, once, but I didn't know what to make of it,
there was nothing straightforward, of course, but it did talk of
the pain . . . I didn't do all I should have
MEPHISTO: you feel guilty?
AGAPE: we always feel guilty, anyhow... Dora had lied
MEPHISTO: lied?
AGAPE: so as not to cause hurt, to protect us, she was impeccable
in her relationships. We were already so worn down, all of us
MEPHISTO: tell me straight, what do you think Dora felt on that
trip?
AGAPE: a shattering, something like a total shattering of hope,
in some ways she'd thought that on that new continent...
then realized that neither there nor anywhere, a shattering,
something like a metaphor, a metaphor of death camps...
MEPHISTO: madame you realize I wasn't there
AGAPE: Dora summed up her horror in an image, thousands
of people eating as they walked, and if we're not yet at that
extreme, if we still use tables and tablecloths, it's just a question
of time. How long might it take us and our "rural paradises"
to swell the numbers of those who can't enjoy the least bit
of relaxation? Dora described a civilization in which cities
completely emptied of their productive function created beings
that drifted toward the soil; in the midst of opulence they

oscillated toward servitude or even more archaic forms of work, archaic to us, but never, ever, toward a hypothetical Nature, beings completely outside distinctions of sex or gender and with no possibility of any access to their own bodies, dispossessed even of the least vestige of control over their working power

MEPHISTO: alienated beings?

AGAPE: absolutely

MEPHISTO: one-dimensional?

AGAPE: no, no, even worse!

MEPHISTO: without attributes?

AGAPE: not even that

MEPHISTO: amnesiac?

AGAPE: it has nothing to do with beings lacking memory, no such category can even describe the horror, Dora Diamant's horror, that's where metaphor comes in, Dora talked of an anaemic civilization, in which the day is much like days in the camps, similar in its effect on people but different in terms of hope, in terms of beliefs about materiality, the materiality of bodies

MEPHISTO: remember my absence, remember the years, the centuries I was gone

AGAPE: what's different is that in this society food, housing, health, even education are secure, which is to say that a person is born and lives in the belief that the world we know will continue and that workers' rights, all the old proletarian conquests we take as given, they're secure, in reality what happens is that you eat but don't eat, you attend school, even university, but you don't attend, you get better but your sickness does not abate, you have fun but you don't have fun, you only think you have fun, a life of phantoms, of beings that can't touch ground

MEPHISTO: someone must run that world

AGAPE: no contacts exist

MEPHISTO: a possibility?

AGAPE: possibility of contamination, of course, in fact we think, sir, that it might interest you

MEPHISTO: that metaphor . . . is it real?

AGAPE: maybe, maybe not, what counts is that someone could think it up, that it could be conceptualized like this, though with the situation not yet that extreme, it's—above all—there in the total absence of hope that real expectations can germinate, take hold from the sheer force of having been created by fusion at the highest temperature, but the configuration of a strategy takes time and Dora had none, the possibility was denied her, in an extremely disconcerting moment, such a situation can provoke someone to disappear, even someone with great powers

MEPHISTO: evil, death, are they still interesting?

AGAPE: absolutely, they abandoned us when you abandoned us, sir, and anyway there's sickness or, more precisely, the ways we survive and live inside sickness

MEPHISTO: could we go on by applying gnostic formulations?

AGAPE: no one would believe it, Simon meeting Helen in a whorehouse and both of them flying over Rome . . . it's role-playing, rhetoric . . . and we're not even talking about "arcane principles" or the serpent that enfolds the world and separates it radically from God, not to mention the wall of fire that is the abyss, nor all those ejaculations the soul learns so as to reach the crystalline-imperial heavens, the ether and all that, those whirlwinds of souls

MEPHISTO: "the Lady," perhaps the Lady could still be of use

AGAPE: what Lady are you talking about?

MEPHISTO: the Oval Lady, one of the six tapestries of the mansion of Saint Germain, in the ancient thermal baths of Lutetia

AGAPE: my knowledge of Christian culture, sir, you must excuse me

MEPHISTO: the Lady is the daughter of light, the clear light of kings abides in her, her gowns . . . the Lady is also a sign of alliance, meaning the Lady of Gerard, of courtly love, that black sun, melancholy, and her jewel-case, we could even open the jewel-case

AGAPE: what do you keep in the jewel-case, sir?

MEPHISTO: death, my darling, death, and the grotesque

AGAPE: we could resuscitate Death?

MEPHISTO: of course we could

AGAPE: sir, will you join our forces?

MEPHISTO: madame, could I really? I've been homeless in the world so many years!

AGAPE: we've got amazing doctors, even I've been reprogrammed

MEPHISTO: reprogrammed?

Agape: yes, a few chips and organs, young organs naturally,
but listen! they're calling us to lunch, in California the food's
excellent as ever

 worse, even worse than my musings aboard a bateau-
mouche, all my disasters, my apocalypses like boeings, nowhere
in any of the galaxies
(the impossible resurrection of Dora Diamant)

 in a thousand shattered CYCLOIDS, such Salamonic
helixes

 (for Manuel Lorenzo)

abracadabra and the mountains open up

February 15th. A withering of the will, or so Marianne thought in front of the rough channels meant to drain the fields, "it'll end up coming in the house," a waning of life. Yet the conditions of her existence weren't that funereal, despite being in full family madness (layers and layers of cerebral bark peeling off in winged whirls), hardly any space for her own thoughts, so her words spy themselves in the green of lichen and the far-off rumble of a tractor; to tell the truth, Marianne wasn't able to think of anything in the universe or
the universe in anything, her thoughts stray, veer off track, no chance whatsoever at any point of contact and all the news, so stubborn, yes, stubborn.

February 17th. Today I'll breakfast with Tobias and Tobias will talk of the Egyptians, of slavery and Louise with eyes like those in the Cairo museum and, me, unconsciously I'll recall the quasi-vegetal hand of some Sumerian or Babylonian or in the metro; of some excavated city forgotten between the stones and how in this city there are so many temples, severe, Ionic, each temple with its architrave, cornices and lintels contains what's prior and first, Paulo Vásquez would say "it's an amalgam of dust" and would even explain how donkeys with delicate step have trod each step of an interminable staircase.
— "Because today (it's cua-Talá speaking) our heart is in Baghdad, beside the tells, at the beginning, despite all the frozen winters."

February 19th. Not even coming close to that word "Bliss," not even coming near, let alone making plans for it. *Promises of any kind of bliss seem hopes for eternal life*, F.K.—don't ever forget these words.

February 26th. London, where all paths cross. Sorrow, the real sorrow of Brenda.

Now Lord Arthur Holmwood, the spiffed-up American gentleman and the doctor all needed rest, precarious, the precarious energy of Lucy. Brenda, her real affliction.
She's already the young woman who bears the mark of gunfire on her forehead in the shape of a sacred seal. Despite the long wait, despite the dike in every ocean, separation is total and the pain acute, irrevocable. *It's these hours that devour our song*, M.L.

I write down events in the story of Mina Murray; all her panic was lodged in the thyroid, between neck and chin, it was there she imagined, in the place to best plunge a dagger, as full of tumors. So she lost her fear of travel, of arriving alone, of getting lost at "the bridge of young mares."
—because it's not the same, when you travel alone you have to take on the world and if you travel with someone, your mind's on that person, and if you're to take on the world, forget it! Already you've no space for yourself, as well as having to pay attention "um, you saw *what*?" Now that I still have my wits about me I'm going to try to pack. KG will take m-Gas for a walk once I'm out of here, once I'm on that trip.

February 27th. Too much agony, way too much; I get this diary mixed up with all other diaries whether or not they're in typewritten signs. The Jews of Bistritz who return to their homes.

February 28th. "Common snipe," 2 a.m., sound of a two-step or something like a two-step; a scrape, twenty seconds—oh what are twenty seconds dancing cheek to cheek!—stop, half a minute. Edith, four days "look at me, nothing bugs me more than someone daydreaming when I talk to him"; she couldn't dance but tried, never mind the grass-stains. Ruined, I'm ruined! My life is a reset button, I always have to go back and reboot, command-control, constantly, that's it, it's all ruined, I'm gonna quit! Yes, I tell you, I quit.

March 2nd. "Mephisto is the memory of my power and of the body's destruction," Raida said, "surpassing the agility of a leopard, the bearing and grace of a deer, the powerful eye of the dragon—it's not exactly that no angel hears me. I'm caught between the memory of my strength and the reduction of the voice in the learning of Language. The odour is decay, sulphur (my blue suede shoes). All my capital is a sun that sets toward the west and the signs of Earth."

Then Raida knew her body was the Sublime "for in it and in equal parts and in balance is the acute shock between the hugest of fortunes and the greatest misfortunes, the absurdity of existence, the riches"
and she knew of the body's destruction by the unbearable weight of the passion of God, by the word
—that this passion led her to an unrelenting desire for disappearance, in the cerebral circumvolutions of time. And so the forest closed upon itself.
That's what's in the writings of the Yawist Bathsheba or the real meaning of "opening toward light" or genesis. In the tomb of Cordelia.
RAIDA: do you know what ice is, by any chance?
RAIDA (her astral body): ice is paralysis of all action, but I, Raida, will deter combustion of the great coagulation so that Hamlet can carry out his crimes and Ophelia braid a crown in the evil power of the waters. There's Hamlet killing rats, there unraveling intimate intrigues, trading luck, fate and name, and there's Ophelia warbling soft songs, carried by the music of the spheres. Hamlet caught in the act of murder,
Ophelia in a dance step.
White hawthorn, flower on the impossible tomb of Cordelia.

Later, father's letters arrive, offering me psychiatric help.

Long live Grimm!

Down with the Eiffelturm!

March 5th. So she dispenses with everything but her own work habits, just between us, vilified, all that's not an interest of hers, personal and the sale of her soul. It happens, oh yes it happens

the pin that probes the heart and clasps you to the world makes of you a compass rose.

She fled metaphor because metaphor disparages the body. It's not easy to hurl away the head of the king, to transform the locks of the queen.

The idea of death impedes her from finishing any exercise, even writing. The idea of dying is, for Elias, very broad and includes his relationship with his spouse

(*I have been forty years wandering from Canaan*), *I look back at it like a foreigner*. F.K.

I have to stop, even for just a moment, take a break from Literature. Arrival in Monforte with María Esteirán: 7 a.m., porn film in the station bar, somnambulant waiters confuse all the returns, all the risings.

Slow reading in the diaries of Kafka

March 7th. Actually the professions, of living just as much as that of being a poet, are in the library, it wasn't a dream at all, beside them is "Bliss", something by Anaïs, Ubu indicative

Vinery. The legacy of Cordelia Diamant. Un-rhymed

"dream of the battle of Lake Maracaibo"

[interrupt here]

March 9th. In that sense, in the sense of an inability and/or refusal to occupy the place of father-Hamlet, prince of Denmark and mirror of all princes; in the sense of Rimbaud, Lautreamont, Lois Pereiro or Manuel Outeiriño, it's totally Kafkaesque. Most "princes" who decide on a literary work are poets, but if Hamlet opts for prose, the stories, letters, diaries, the novels of Kafka would be his. To say that Kafka, even though he's contemporary with our great-grandfathers, is a literary father is an error that Kafka himself would view with disgust, Kafka at best is a brother, an excellent brother, and at worst, a lover, a lousy and dolorous lover too. To imagine Kafka and Lautréamont crossing the Praza da Quintana at night, what a good idea. My weakness for K., and for Hamlet Prince of D., mirror of spellbound princes. With a few notable differences, for K. reached immortality through his works, and Hamlet we remember for his wavering, for his crimes and above all for the stupid fact of dying. The vanity of Hamlet, the humility of Kafka, the scale tips in favour of the second, for it surpasses the first in its clear view of self and loving generosity. It's as if through constant striving to supercede his own weakness, Kafka managed to overtake Hamlet and thus place himself at the level of Shakespeare. In this sense, the prince becomes citizen and reaches a place, unstable but possible, in the world. (The stones of Quintana, gladioli, calyxes, illness—certain psychic aches—, harmonicas, ships' bows, silicosis, but above all melancholy, a passion for the East and theosophical or Atlantic-mystical societies are princely attributes along with a non-disdainable capacity for logical thought.) I think too of Wittgenstein, the house he built for his sister in Vienna now occupied by an embassy of a distant Eastern country. All are extraordinarily beautiful. Perhaps in the 20th century thanks to the efforts of Franz, today's inhabitants can take root in this ruined world, not exactly to take the place of the father but with thanks to certain advances in medicine [interrupt here]

Then the voice outside all vocal articulation: the body of Erzsébet Báthory.

EMINIA *(princess captive in the borderlands of Zamora):* the image of a cosmos with planets all harmonically spinning blurs all or any of my ideas. A drop of God, hybrid, hybrid with you, o "Great Alien."
(From the notes of Doctor Roberta Dehmen, phonographically recorded): Soul that constantly unravels, soul wrapped in its down, in the oval netting of Erzsébet Báthory.

JONAS: Hey everyone! Quick now, where could the Count have counted up the husks crushed by the sword. Olaf, over here! I'm Ophelia, the Danish lass, I decipher runes, zigzag on skis, finger the harp and sprain my groin. I Bridgid, Birgitta Birgersdotter: all my "Revelations," even the most extravagant, were translated all or in part into every language of significance. I Reguilda, deprived for four years of sight in my left eye. I Gide, "item ad Sanctum Iacobum tres solidos sterlingorum." The Lady we'll put right here; and will the Queen's hair be grey, silver like her tapestries? Will her skeleton be kept for us to admire in some museum?
Four hearts plus one that no mirror can catch.
Strip off and dance, Inglinga answered, I watched that lute, is paradise ever green! Will I wear rough-cut sealskin panties, and on my helmet a walrus skinned alive? I'll wrap myself in a caftan trimmed in sibylline marten, ski in the swan-yard, the tiny ski of Ati.

EMINIA: poetic material the resuscitated
brother dresses me and draws the garden of childhood in filigree. Look, flowers, hermetic in refrigerated chambers: locoweed, boletus, casablanca lilies. I cloaked the perfect radio of my absence.

DEHMEN: Jonas thinks he's Jonas and that his word's the word of God and his dreams the dreams of God. These are the words of Jonas, words he believes between white cloud and heavenly constellation. In his worn-down state of health, he really believes he possesses all these voices.

DEHMEN: I try to make him realize he's in no danger, but he hides papers, an acute anxiety attack, finally confesses that the astral ghost of a young woman poet in a future time will have to plagiarize his argument and what's worse, turn herself into Galatea. Half an hour later he's still shouting. Insists he doesn't know what I'm talking about. A very worrying situation.

HOMUNCULUS-HERMAPHRODITE: mermaids or, rather, mermaid skeletons: Dorians or, rather, the three Graces of the Sea, 1/10-millionth of one of my blood cells, star-shaped in a test tube. Shipwrecks

(Dr. Alveiros pops up again)

JONAS: But what was she doing there, in the dunes, under a parasol of stars? so ancient, in bikini and chipped nail polish, her pamela hat sculpted like a nest of owlets—as if the owl'd flown off at dusk—was she awaiting death? awaiting a patronymic hero, stupid and defunct, to chop her head from her torso? and if so, why was her price an ingot of alchemical gold? why did she sing, while distilling litres of gin, songs from her youth? was that sea the Styx? while California burned and Eurydice, young Eurydice, set off. And Penthesileia, was Penthesileia a man? what sort of man? Achilles a woman? Blond Marilyn, and Tancredo, and Clorinda? Four will be the number of my progenitors.

DEHMEN: I walk in and out of the text like you'd saunter in and out of spring. My words are Jonas' words, are Olaf's. I don't recognize the world. I write down the "madhouse." "And with crisscrossed oars, we forge through an enormous and agitated sea and the abyss full of monsters"

JONAS: If you drink the limit, you're in the deluge. Purity. Purity can't be established. The book's of chance. In chance is the

Infinite. If you drink the deluge. If you drink the dove. If you drink the Ark, both Ark and promise. And the children of Noah and the vines—ogresses existed—

—thou shalt make an Ark and behold I do thee bring a deluge and it was the 17th day of the second month, and the waters lifted the Ark upon the mountaintop

—I will set out a rainbow the exact candles of the solstice
You know me well! . . . if you devour the poem, if you mistake it for a sarcophagus, for the mummy of Tutankhamun. If you wrap yourself in papyrus. If you roll yourself in it.
NEBAMUN: all praise to the dead
—you mount the fire, inside is Sigrid, in the house of conflagration

EMINIA: you stay at the side of God, in his amniotic fluid
JONAS: for we know each other without carpeting the jungle the pent-up reservoir of gardenias
DEHMEN: so many people to kill, I don't have enough time!
Mother Nature.

Farewell, Lyric!

Marquis- Au revoir, Manchuria!

Ticket found in Dr. Alveiros' pocket *(reading by Doctor Dehmen):* It is with pleasure that Messrs. Swedenborg Otero, Allan Kardec Risco and Daniel Blavatsky, members of the "Bony Architecture, the machine hums without a motor" Association, invite you to an aquatic acrobatic masked ball to be held on the 17th of the present month at midnight in the Great Hall of the Lyceum. Black tie requested. The music will transcend any known fantastical symphony. We offer the presence, already confirmed, of distinguished ladies Hatshepsut and Nefertiti, freed at last from their bandages thanks to the prayer circle created by Dr. Alveiros. The Great Chooboo, our choreographer, will direct the scene. Buses and trains will depart from the usual places.

Note: We will make sure we put everything back in its place when we're done, each in its own tomb, and of course we won't mix up the living and the dead.

Your most aff. sv. & u.l.f.

The President

Arthur, dear: The logotype! At last we get to a waking dream of little Orbilius: Orbilius surrounded by swans and doves is visited by a god, Apollo writes on his forehead TU VATES ERIS

Orbilius reappears before his mother,
his native, materno-biological mother, But you believe in materno-biological languages?
labra labellis, a kiss of love, putrid, perfect

the kiss of Orbilius, as you can imagine, represents the young poet's impossible reconciliation with his mother. This "mother" refers not only to his own biological mother but to the culture of origins itself and naturally to language; the Latin language that, mixed with older substrates gave form, in the heat of invasions, to communication devices that reign even today across a good expanse of European geography. This "mother," Europe, her languages: this putrid "kiss," perfect, Christian. The poet flees. So this will be the "logotype"

of course at the age of eight I couldn't imagine life in the desert, nor in the jungle, nor on the savanna—I had no encyclopaedia—nor did I bite the little brute, I mean the workers' daughter, in the ass.
But yes I had the *Wonderful Adventures of Antipher* and an atlas for measuring longitudes and latitudes, and Cleopatra, in the imperial court of Cleopatra; evil:

evil is mass culture. Evil is something intended for consumption —
the taste for crime and its tidy academic representations,
the glorious resurrection of bodies mixed in the desires of Nina-Elizabeta. Her pornography. Evil is this market alienated from the passions.
Idiocy in the language

the girl-child; this child is a poet girl abandoned

je suis le saint
je suis le savant
je suis le piéton
je suis bien l'enfant abandonné

she feels someone's been here first. Outside around her is
"Nature and the Peasant Idyll"; she couldn't give a hoot

> later I'll encounter other topoi of the century: the great
> universal exhibitions, Luna Parks, Rimbaudian orphéons of
> the future

> a colonial era, Arthur! an era of colonies

> stony ache, gift of languages. Hegel and female orgasm
> —the spirit oh I see it every morning reviving in the garden
> the brutal song of Margarida: that dead lad who smashed
> her lips as once he smashed inside her
> may they disguise themselves, as Ophelia, as Margarida, go
> mad, may they go mad, may these women go insane in the
> mental wards: the case of Dora
> Dead lips of the mother, lips of literary language

Margarida: co-protagonist of the Tragedy of Faust. The "brutal song
of Margarida": the love song or lullaby Margarida intones, already mad
and jailed, after having "murdered" the child of her relations with Faust.
Margarida represents, in the European tradition, the "eternal feminine"

"may they disguise themselves, as . . .": therapeutic practice once used in
mental wards. You can consult a bibliography, even look at colotypes
— Hugh Welch Diamond, Surrey Asylum, 1842, with period
photographs
— Réguard Salpêtrière, Charcot Archive, etc.
— The "case of Dora" is Dora, of course: "Fragmentary Analysis of a
Case of Hysteria."

"Commerçant! Colonist! Medium!"
Go be the Messiah!

who free of the rebellions of Logic . . .

grey, huge, impenetrable. I can't even imagine the years
right after the civil war, nor the repression: the war

the girl is born here, in this grey. Relief
I write about this girl

the girl is curious, rummages in the box of photographs,
those not in any album: "from that utter hell." And she figures out
"that hell" is not the one painted in the roadside shrines

classroom on the left, symmetrically identical: the children here
don't have haircuts like her friend's, they've shaved heads, to the
quick. Impossible site of representation,
the girl inspects the milk-bin, this milk, white, powdered

like in catechism, where you never feel good even if they pin the
ribbon on you because something's always going on with your
stockings

like in unending torture, noon mass at the parish church; of her
father who always has something going on with his shoes, of all the
fathers, with their shoes, their ties, their shirts. Like the mothers,
no one's to know but they're all popping phenobarbs, so: rosy

the grandmother denies the grey, the shiny surface of things
the grandmother is a force of nature
and has a truck, a beauty

like the father's cousins, all of them left with others, who come
and go all over the world, to Argentina, Caracas, Germany, to
Barcelona, the Basque country, to the planets

like Olympia in the port city of summers; it's clear they killed her
boyfriend. The girl figures out that his death wasn't simply that,
it's a crime, murder and even worse because they shaved Olympia's
hair—as they did to the charity pupils—and tore off her doorplate,
because she'd worked on the Statute of Autonomy; the girl doesn't

know what the Statute is but Olympia has books, many books, and when she's fourteen Olympia will let her use the Library. Then she'll know what kind of thing the Statute is.

and about Uncle Manolo who was kept hidden; the girl can't understand how he could have been kept hidden, where?

the girl is eight, walks with her father on a grey day, winter, enters the Lyceum, a warm place, safe; she understands absolutely nothing said there, fascinated with her father's attention, the salon so ornate, fascinated with words: Don Ramón Otero Pedrayo speaks, will speak, speaks, so she learns, learns then, the *Pedra*.
Pedra, Stone, means identity, hers, her city's, cubic, perfect

at the age of eleven, this girl knows all there is to know
        the stone refutes the grey
        the stone refutes the surface glitter

this girl who now walks into a salon, spacious, a ballroom, who looks out and sees every one of you, sires
the girl who recites: *red, yellow, purple*
and knows that tonight the Stone will refute once and forever the odious *Fallen for God and Country*, in every church, in all the absolute horror of childhood
in her incredible misfortune

grey, huge, impenetrable

> stone refutes the grey, constructs the language of Utopia, language that dispenses with the ordinary language of business, the extraordinary language of salvation, the singular one of "dark misfortune." Poem that constructs itself upon an "us," nation-community: *Lineage*, X.L.M.F.

You keep thinking about idiocy,
about mathematics, even.

About utopia:

Who free of the rebellions of Lyric will not be . . .

end stop, Arthur! Pandora's box

ver erat et morbo Romae languebat inerti Orbilius

a writing pained, biological, native: excruciating!

Ada, gulf of Aden, in Abyssinia.

my relations with the Marquis: some time ago we abandoned all
philosophy of the toilet, and Justine as theoretical-philanthropical
model. As for the rest, Isidore! . . .

Arithmetic! Algebra! Geometry! Grandiose triad!

Luminous triangle!

Ada: Ada Leis Paris, literary facsimile of the *Daughter of the Sea*
(Rosalía de Castro, Galicia, 1837–1885) who according to a manuscript,
certainly apocryphal, found by the author, does not meet her demise amid
native cliffs, but after many and diverse adventures settles in Louisiana
as rich and moneyed heiress. She sponsors construction of the "Albert
Ansont de Gramont" Orphanage or "Foundation" along with Lois Pereiro
and Isidore Ducasse, the Comte de Lautréamont, author of *Les Chants* (Je
te salue, vieil océan), in Caribbean lands

"Albert Ansot de Gramont" Orphanage: refuge for boy and girl
poets where they're taught, in line with modern theories of literary
communication, that the "Lyric" subject of enunciation does not
coincide, and even less each day, with the subject that writes. And further:
this subject is decidedly the result of the linguistic copula between the
"familial novel" and the "community novel," which is exactly the same as
affirming that this "I" coincides with "the green shining coast" or "Allons
Enfants de la patrie!"

in short: the modern lyric revolution is not a way of experiencing
oneself, of sounding the depth of one's inner life nor, on the other hand,
of plunging the self into the depths of nature. It is, first of all, a specific
mode of enunciation, a way of accompanying what is uttered in the
poem, of deploying it in perceivable space, of rhyming it in a walk, a
voyage, a crossing [...]

a new political experience of the perceptible or perceptual experience of the political . . .

Rancière, Jacques. *La chair des mots : Politiques de l'écriture.* Paris: Galilée, 1998.

the poet, she gets all emotional, like more and further landscapes unfolding. Fourth voyage of the third prostitute of Qumran or sands that Mandelstam desired

because I hear my voice in another and another voice, in another such tiny trees

—nationalism is a question of identity, they rob you of your identity, because that identity can't really exist, and you suffer all your life from the theft, trying to get restitution from them, staring straight at the thieves and trying to make them do you justice. The rebuilding of this identity, its impossible reconstruction, are the history of the nation, history of the poem

I'm self-cryogenating
in this non-place: tundraGnawed-opening

Enshamanize yourself
and flourish me.

(for Helena González)

access to the head dangling by its hair or
the memoirs of Doctor Roberta Dehmen (never sent anywhere)
Tiger-Shulamith, mutant, metacorporeal
Selenite

(part two)

Dr. Dehmen-Mutant, Mermaid chorus: it's not that I feel I'm
just starting; as far my artistic ability goes, I biologically precede
the point when I engendered myself
Dr. Dehmen-Mutant, chorus of Gorgonas: I become the
woman who saw no one in my clinic, yet the entire species is
waiting for me there. I'm writing of a time when I was not a
poet, that other time, in my head
Dr. Dehmen: what's key is not how I create the poem but to
be able to interpret it in a given direction. Thus the pearl, to
enter the pearl and experience all the fractures of the sea. And
Ada, how can we create the after-life in which she heads with
her father, newly rich, to Louisiana. Ada's encounter with
the "Mathematical Sublime," the founding of the "Ansot de
Gramont" Orphanage, the strategy for Maracaibo, Oliverio de
Clissont and the great princes of the sea.
Ada survives, far deeper than 20,000 leagues voyaged under the
sea.
Dr. Dehmen-Mutant, Mermaid chorus: what you can't
stand is the death of the heroine, so you grant her a gift of
transformation, gift of life. Ophelia, daughter of the sea, I am
the time in which you're not a poet. Long live whoever sucks the
waves from the sea!
Dr. Dehmen: what attracts us about Erzsébet Báthory is the
impossibility of her desire, that impossibility of submitting to
any civilized standard, her withdrawal. Erzsébet is the total
promiscuity of feminine bodies, the delirium of an absence, a

possession without limits.

For Goethe the erotic was in the voice, for Calderón it was
an optic of the senses, neither demands anything different or
particular from their own head.

The dread of night, shuddered waves, treasure swallowed in the
shipwreck.

Sade, the philosopher, overcomes them in a lucky combo of the
four elements.

That the dead excite you, the severed heads of the dead, that loop
or node in the nerve system of night, corresponds to the need to
eliminate the line between life and death.

Breathe! Hold your breath! Exhale! Her pulmonary cells instantly
ready.

The swans once more devoured by the current.

You take pleasure in the body's interaction in the spell of a scene:
forty years it took to resolve the incest, the delicacy of the brother,
your jealousy at his birth

DR. DEHMEN-MERMAID: a god that engenders himself and while
ever himself fails to recognize himself

She-Cosmic sleeps upon the waters

Jonas the ventriloquist botches the prophecy, as in the farces of
Proteus

Will you tell us your story?

GORGONA: in his fatherly desires, Nereo only has eyes for Galatea

DR. DEHMEN: my shadow, being a gnomon, chants the hours in
the waters of the pond

GORGONAS: suddenly intimate, we abandon all "public business,"
in the sense that we abandon ownership of monuments and
landscapes

MERMAIDS: we feel ourselves mistresses of the visible

DR. DEHMEN: we enter God's cupola, beatitude in the face of snow

MERMAIDS: she-Petrea, thinking she's the rockface, the sweep of
her shawl

GORGONAS: hymentalia, abyss

DEHMEN: it opens like a double-headed axe, like a cavern

MERMAIDS: and the ship, glows in the middle, in the bay

GORGONAS: ship, sinister

MERMAIDS: the heads of the lovers severed and a heart pierced
GORGONAS: water-lily and lacustrine celery
MERMAIDS: 80 miles off the Guinea coast
like lead, we sank in a steamship,
butterflies and bindweed on both banks and mahogany in the
rainforest
and tourists watching the glacier crack and icebergs calve
and thousands of penguins, sea-lions and seals with gleaming
pelts
MERMAIDS: to weave the sea, the oval, the ellipse
DEHMEN: rather, to reflect the dream, that they came back, that
they were returning, mutilated bodies, in trucks, people at the
roadsides, in the ditches
MERMAIDS: and a pain as old as exploitation, as labour, as undue
appropriation of the forces of labour, as women kept from the
public scene, as the appropriation of their productive forces
DEHMEN: so far away, on the horizon
MERMAIDS: then it was the end, the pages of a book
GORGONAS: the gentleness of the animal waking in my arms
DEHMEN: once more: the fever of dead roads, in the symbolic
itinerary of the street, in the lying fortune-teller
MERMAIDS: for we rapidly arrive at a horizontal burrow and just
as fast our eyes get used to the darkness, we're plunged in it,
where the sea gurgles, salt sea of tears and the birds came even
here and the journey was accompanied by a melodious chirp—"I
hate you!"—in remote bedrooms, at the orbiting compass, star.
And to think we could put an end to sickness and death, ensure
all on earth can live in dignity and health, let those who love
each other stay together always
GORGONAS: take advantage of it, criminal of the altar!
MERMAIDS: later rodents will suture my veins, flowers of
impossible referents
DEHMEN: his way of impatiently tapping metal against the
marble of the bar, right by the telephone and coins; I knew I'd
have no choice but to satisfy the desire in his breast, the extreme
dryness of his, awaiting a rape, but I had no tongue. He tapped
into me so as to turn into her, into speech, into everything. Light

to decapitate light, through identical self-representations, of he himself, to you.

Corrupt eyes of language, lethal

Mutant metacorporeal head of Dr. Dehmen: how many of us women have spent our hours of leisure or daydream drawing just such labyrinths?

Gorgonas: viscerae, in which it's easy to lose one's way at certain times, in certain ways of seeing life, 20 km of paths, bifurcations and dead-end alleys. We'll bathe ourselves in our brother's blood, we're again abandoned

Mermaids: his tigers, his lynxes soaring over the seas

Gorgon: a heavenly constellation, solar vortex, dance

Mermaids: we'll wrap his cherished viscerae round us, keep them in stems of crystal, we'll make jams, feasts, charms, delicacies

all the balls of thread will be purple

like carmine, frozen

Arachnida: thus our wandering will be the infinite refraction of a ray of light in the labyrinthine meld of mirrors

Mermaids: to project emblems and bouquets of flowers, ties to eternity, links to life

Arachnida: gardenias and orchids of new worlds and far-off tulips of madness

melancholy gardens where Porphyry, Hypatia and Iamblicus play

Mermaids: love will string its garlands beneath the celestial vault

Dr: you're all talking of Philosophy?

Mermaids: no, of gallantry

of shady plants beneath the demands of reason and aspirations of fantasy

Arachnida: an inclination of the spirit toward nature's voices

Mermaids: to hear the fairies' song

Arachnida: in the computer sector in general

Mermaids: in modern anti-aircraft batteries

Arachnida: in a plethora of missiles

Mermaids: in the great complexes of programming

Arachnida: even in modern architecture

MERMAIDS: neither Baroque nor Hellenistic, Buddhist nor Hindu but all of it simultaneously

ARACHNIDA: we'll get to the centre, if we think centripetal

MERMAIDS: we'll leave amiably, if we think centrifugal

ARACHNIDA: we're zooming in on the medulla, then withdrawing further each time

MERMAIDS: from this solid and imperial place

ARACHNIDA: two columns four times, two hemispheres separated by the chirp of a bird, we start to spin

MERMAIDS: clockwise and counter-clockwise, what savage wind! we twist in a tornado, in spirals we spin

SELENITE: an egg, sire, a speeding egg! seems it has landing problems

CHORUS OF SELENITES: open, sesame! she-Matrix in the core of huge stones, how beautiful. how wonderfully it unfolds while the mountain opens and the two hemispheres separate

GORGON: she's an actress, like Rita, Marlene or Marilyn

MERMAIDS: like us?

GORGON: well, more a therapy

MERMAIDS ah!

DR: what tepid waters! especially after a night of bliss, blissful and restorative, as restorative as the act we celebrate today has the power to heal our wounded eyes frightened from reading inscriptions in churchyards, and miraculous; your presence among us makes and proves the whispers real, tales of the wildest of our clandestine lives, of the memories transmitted in that horror. So let's toast the new configuration of the nation which can only be a federal state within the Third Republic. To your health, girls, my comrades!

GUEST (MALE): wait a second, how are we going to have anything in common? besides, my language is Oestryminian, is the real language, that of petroglyphs

GUEST, STYLISH YOUNG WOMAN: but who today can guarantee me eternity? above all in a country in which no institution bothers to preserve manuscripts?

GUEST, LANGUAGE OF THE EYES: come hither!

DR: Up with Cuba! Long live Fidel Castro!
CHORUS OF SELENITES: in the next chapters

it goes on, it goes on

DR: "Learnèd Conferences on Symbol and Metaphor or
Allegory and Metonymy, in the New Era of Galactico-Electronic
Communications":
MEPHISTO: without a periphery, how can you tell where the edge
of the centre is?
AGAPE: it's jagged, and drops off
MEPHISTO: you're describing me a homogeneous reality that
doesn't allow any visible dissent, any opposition
AGAPE: death and language, selected languages
DEATH: love me, protect me, be my wife
MEPHISTO: where all is marginal with respect to this occupation,
there'd still be a fragile textuality, an allegorical design, anti-
authoritarian, that can't be attracted to the centre, a design
subject to time's deterioration, metonymical
AGAPE: which gives it access to history, the continual mutability
of thought; not the materiality of the word but the carnality of
the poem
MEPHISTO: a displacement of metaphor and symbol?
AGAPE: rather, their exclusion, a complete metaphorization
of the language so no one can dialogue with the father, his
metaphors, his symbols, with his essence
MEPHISTO: a world practically incontestable
AGAPE: you might say that
THE AUTHOR, SHE: love of lichen, the fire of a tiny tree, a carpet
of moss . . . Mother! Hold me up with your body, the wind's
inclement in the word
OPHELIA: what counts is not to be or not to be Ophelia, what
counts is not weaving a crown for one's own death
MERMAIDS: we won't renounce the passions, but yes we'll alter
this story's course
OPHELIA: my hands are freezing! don't mention philosophers to
me and don't remind me of poets either; forget the whole lot of

them!

MERMAIDS: dumbstruck in an idea while time speeds past

PHILOSOPHERS: for millennia even, trying to resist the poem's seduction

DEATH: kiss me! if you don't, I'll kiss you

OPHELIA: even Margarida went crazy. Henry! You scare me. We'll change the way the song goes

> "The one who killed me
> was my mother, the whore!
> And the falsity of my father
> was what devoured me!
> My little sister
> gathered my bones
> in some airy spot
> then turned me
> into a pretty birdie
> who through the forest flies far, far away"

MERMAIDS: the intestinal flora of monsters colonizes and fertilizes the soil. Those flashes under the tundra are the pale dawn of the cultural imperium, majesty of future days

THE AUTHOR, SHE: you always have to prove to me that the world can be created anew in writing, can be intellect, forest, modernity, meaning, shade and waves

"O waves of the sea at Vigo"

MERMAIDS: amber like some trinket of the Count's

ARACHNIDAS: like some salubrious portrait of Shakespeare

GORGON: tesserae of emotion

MERMAIDS: ancient houseguests

ARACHNIDAS: now that you know all about alchemical sperm

GORGON: about metempsychosis

MERMAIDS: about the Bomarckian turn

ARACHNIDAS: Homunculus will be born!

GORGON: in the glow of Artemis

MERMAIDS: Barca! Diana! Hecate!

DR. DEHMEN-SPOKESWOMAN: young poets of both sexes all agree these days on the non-existence of Being in the post-biological fabric of contemporary language. Having sprung out of the Earth's depths, maybe they're the result of their various conversations and suggestive poetic genres
Or how to apply new techniques of genetic engineering to talented cells or genetic pattern or to the cellular chaos in modern post-contemporary poetry.

She-Transformation gets lost in O'Hare Airport

your gaze follows the truck, white, hermetic, with no mark or identifying sign

To the springtime of peoples!

GENESIS
GENESIS
GENESIS
nature

the author, she = Tigridia Shulamith

Casablanca, May, 1950*

* note: the author assumes no responsibility for opinions dished out by the various voices in this text or in any other published under her name.

or in a rush. In my all-consuming rush at Delphi to get to some café: dark curls, Dunhill. Home of dioramas. Almost as if there were a slight family relation, as if you were reading the Poem. About the *flipper* woman. About the woman furled in a Manila shawl. Someone reads, someone is shadow, someone wears my grandmother's watch, how geese flock together, apple tree and dovecote! And her earrings dangling.

You'll say:

—I'm a woman who wears sea and comet under distant trees HOUSES OF LOVE

For it's a secret the Father can share only with the girl. The girl is always disguised.

—cages! That's what my father prepared: little tombs.

She's the woman on whom every knife has carved. Words of ice. Words we carried with us across the Rhine, that they can't even imagine

—ripened to gold

Like a lover we no longer desire but from whom we still crave torment, or at least that his happiness not be fully satisfied. Besides, I don't remember his hair. He doesn't remember it, that's certain. In the realm of cauldrons. With star clusters budding from the sky. Scene of tumult. My dearest sir: please let me express my opinion on this page. It's been a long time, years maybe, since our relationship slowly and inexorably deteriorated. And since you sire moved, it crumbles like the hulk of an abandoned ship. So you think, you think and you start to look. You think you're an executive secretary and must kiss his feet, then he pushes you to your knees and fucks you from behind. You think you're a secretary seeking work in the offices of a top executive, then he pulls up your pleated miniskirt and fucks you from behind. You think you're one of seven sisters and he likes you best and loves you nightly in his hotel bed. Then you take off.

You take off in total bliss, euphoric. Empty. No writing, no love.
The place where no one writes. The price. Ixion. Till he breaks
into tears. They contemplate the valley. Step on every vertebra
of the building. They don't hug. I want to hug you. A nearly
desperate gesture.
—it's breathtaking! the contortionist's dangling rings
You'll say:
—I'm a woman who spent her wedding night where they
filmed *The Third Man*. On the Orient Express, in nightclubs, at
the desert edge. And the voice that opens, in the body: born.
Voice that skips in the ruins which are twelve rings of fire. Skin,
so white. Letter to Abdul Bande-Noire: the second one I write
him. I can't feel empathy. This feeling that at some point we are
excluded from language.
That violence. You were on the verge of happiness. This letter
is the tale of an extenuation, of an extinction of Language
between you and me—what matters is not if we still love
each other, if you sire still desire me—what matters is your
renunciation, renunciation of the power of speech, of
communicating. I have to insist.

(with Amelia Gamoneda)

what wind whistles in your garden? which is the ardent necessity of your night? what do you know? girl, are you condemned? falling? do the pale stars of fear flee? do you know of the Creator? do you know his desire? are you OK? under what maternal breast? what do you want of me? dances with the leaves and the pleasure of summer? what are you doing in this city? do you desire my life, my gazelle life, my antelope life? do the spheres intone a funereal lament? for you? do winds whistle in the city of the dead? wrest light from your life? are your eyes clear as *arrugiums*? was sadness a guest in your home? fatigue burn you out? will you breathe my soul, breathe the eternal? are you sick of all the heavens? do you murmur in the woods and the garden of silver? are you my favourite buffoon? are you savage as the sun? will you kiss the pulse of my fiery viscerae, my avalanche of snow? you watched the sky? I love you. I love you. you chose me? are these the colours of your soul? must I think of you? do nights grow in your head? do you know where we're going? silence, does your voice ring of silence? will we meet again? do you avert your eyes before me? are your eyes played out? what aroma captivates you? will my heart soar at your fountains? will you rouge my heart? will you paint your lips with the red of clouds? will you remember me? will our dreams fall to earth?

Our ascension
perfect.

(*with Else Lasker-Schüler*)

for Cecilia Dreymüller

it's Fanny, of Kapital-Cosmopolis, lighting up a Murati.
The speed that shrinks all schemata. Trees gently flower and
auras are serene! Nights in Tunisia. Kissing your ankles and
thousands of sundews, one after another. Asfagnum. Like a
kind of omission, distraction, forgetting. Sun and all the rites of
night are still needed, even more. On the 10th of September, the
swallows leave, no one touches them, no one can touch them.
On deck. And schools of fish move in dream. A dream saddened,
of separation, illness, death:
near rocks in a beautiful Bauhaus-animal of ash across the West.
But
the UTERUS, the real uterus, the grail, cauldron, none of them,
not even the Old Patriarch, can put their hands on it. Higher
than bird-flight, cradled in cherry. The poem speaks for itself.
Volcano lithographs. A plot of land with volcano view. The seer
said you'd be a widow, that your brother would die, that after
the age of 28 all would go better, stupendously well. You think:
here we are! A deep valley in the deepest of millennia. Because
yesterday I'd read some info and the hashish made me think the
bass player was an old boyfriend, the carbide-factory guy, and
I mixed up a woman onlooker with the psychologist linked to
Trakl. And so you blew it. You blew it and confused the abyss
with the abyss. Even if you write with purple ink, or with Blue
Florida, or with South Seas. And how to test the stair, on the
hill's brow where sheep wander, one day I went away, took the
Rabal road toward Escornabois, toward Vilaseca. Farewell to all
my dead! Nothing else for it, they rebuild the mill. All the old
movie houses boarded up. The cinemas of love. Outside the
language, outside language. The sundew slowly shuts upon the
trusting mole. The fish, no, they swim. No one knows what it
is fish do. Except by questioning, deriving from context. Maybe
in this way we might know what on earth it is fish do. There's
no financial district or industrial park out there. They work in
the cannery. Lots of elder trees. A Berber carpet designates the

notion of matrimony. They discuss current factory conditions. Are there extractors or no, are there still broken plates or scapulae, now, in the best of current conditions. The wail of wind. Outside language. There's no bear at all in the square, it slopes, writes without margins, is baroque. You never enter at the same spot. Never get ahead. Between cabbage fields. This is how I spend my time, I furnish houses. I do it to get the furniture from my house into my parents', sometimes you're alive. The "malediction," though structural, didn't take place, for it happened earlier, and never again. "You'll never succeed if you don't give in." Incapable of conceiving a multitude of penises. Because I wouldn't get there, he'd shunt me aside. To grab the suitcases, yes, for you go down with the same people you flew up with, but later you go out, so I'd just stay put, shunted aside: True, I could make an effort, call a cab, but in reality I wouldn't get there, just stay put, like the suitcases.

tiger

ANDREA: the tigers are women, but with our hair pinned up in a lovely cap with earflaps of fake leopardskin
we inhabit an embolus
MELBA: um, and the skin?
ANDREA: the skin's an apron, really, you just tie it in front, cross the strings below your breasts, two Grecian armatures, that's what is visible. But when they enter, the bachelors. So subtle, the petal, between dining rooms of fire
JULIE: no way! we don't need an animal-trainer; the air close, unbreathable, the cage becomes a giant glass cylinder, we're in a test-tube or hypodermic syringe; then myriads, or lysergic, and we go blind. And the trapezes, gardens, flower-beds all crumble: vault-womb. Poisonous shoots of yew invade us, and the wolf's canyons, and the cherry and apple trees choked with holly. Ours is a fallen sex. Gabrielle d'Estrées and the Duchesse de Villiers
ANDREA: they pillage you and spread out your arms, flying arms then your veins burst and you start to bleed (you're like this 15 minutes or more). Clearly, it takes a lot of women, but they have to be orphans, in orphanages they knot the rope around your neck and in one hand you've a trowel and you have to be quick for when he runs and kicks out the stool, you have to cut the rope or you died. If you didn't die, you fall, fall from three metres up and so you repeat:
you spread out your arms, FLYING ARMS,
you tie off the string, tighten the tourniquet,
drops splatter over the tiles, infiltrate the perfect dome of the convent of Cluny, in the rugged heights of Candán. You knot Language round your forearm, the weight of the Idiom, snaps on the brown back
of the horses

JULIE: that's where those guys put their money, put it there because you're inside, in the machine of chance, in delicate flounces of white lace and laced red Louis XV shoes of suede and spike heels
MADAME: don't eat the apple, girls, we'll stay on in Eden, in the Harem, in the Circus, the Bordello
four shall be your progenitors
the damsel and death
the woman cannonball
the martyress and the dragon
ALL: we are
THE WONDERS OF THE WORLD IN LIVING COLOUR,
eternal visions of love, the key to the city, perpetual motion
MARGOT: gaze with the colours of reality upon the most meaningful
experience a girl can have
"Mary and the Archangel", manual for those who can't focus on loving ecstasy. Sub fluminis and leopardskin
JULIE: Because you can't speak when you're making love, nor beg for world peace when you're ready for orgasm!
Ommmmm
MADAME: how they torment you, peel back her skin

AUTHOR (SHE): women, caught in their pinball machines, without hymen.

> "the roof covers me like a tangle of serpents"
> David P. Iglesias

flashes of lightning enter and a gentle chill, tender, and on the
china, on everyone's plate (those who are there eating). You eat
bone: chrysanthemum-bone, bone. Do you still have to point out
that the walls of this house are oval? and the children, who follow
ancestral rites, foreshortened against sunset, who have green
marijuana dreams seeded in the grandparents' garden. Veins,
factory of puffy red lips. So swirling, these veins: for millennia.

> "From Princess Chechenit'sya to Count Jan Potocki,
> both travelling out to the steppe"

CHECHENIT'SYA: I tell you that a land without bandits is a
monotonous land, bored, you want to compare? A stolen scarf is
far more thrilling than a gift of pearls. Ever since the world's been
world, the princes of my family have robbed at the Tiflis road or
the Tarku crossing; I'd never want my parents or friends to know
I'd lain with a man who didn't live by banditry.

AUTHOR (SHE): dryads, there they are, dryad crown! and their
forehead and palms of their hands and their sex, how humid the
dark trees are.

REPLICA: at the sound of the hymn, the labourers hunch over.
Their shoulders set awkwardly and their backs curve. Their eyes.
As if a wolf heard hymns or consciousness of the sacred

AUTHOR (SHE): from every age, from every stone, stone of granite,
in front of the forest. Nutrition, into humid roots, into the
ground, into earth

REPLICA: then Chechenit'sya, at the Astrakhan extremity of the
world, right when the Padrón traders bite their louis d'or. SHE-
WOLF galloping into the solstice

ADOSINDA: princesses don't write, unless they're priestesses;
it's not hard to imagine their Chaldean skirts, eyes lengthened
with kohl, their offerent attitude: Judea

because they were two, twins,
from one and the same uterus,
here, where the forest turns red
all sorts of hydraulic machines, near the spores.
AUTHOR (SHE): so I prepare the calendar
REPLICA: this clay, this foliage
on the far side of its genetic code, my body roils in this
coagulation.
AUTHOR (SHE): embryo not of a-God.
So we'll manage to save the lives of ducks and we'll keep on
loving Taj-Mahal birds
smiling at women
REPLICA: what'll I do now with the head, where will I set it, now
that the world grows and the fount multiplies?
AUTHOR (SHE): fever of the beloved dead because rapidly you start
to imagine a name on the gravestones, a name he'd never again
utter, strata upon strata of linguistic registers, archeological, it's
this, this, what the young woman does in the crags of Pitões,
croons to cattle, but you're still mesmerized, watching the scale
in the centre of the room, dumbstruck, weighing kilos and more
kilos, tons of potatoes. Held in that cryptogram. On the balcony,
leaning over the traffic on the highway to Madrid, across all the
Antipher-maps, the Hallstatt planispheres, in the Kunsthistorisches
Museum collections, in a lost-Bernhard page.
Then you traverse the tumultuous Aurach
REPLICA: the mill still smokes on the steppes, a wide carpet and the
herons killed. And the days are thin,
our dance stiff over the river. Worms leap at you. I begin to be
nothing
dispersion to the four winds

                                                    Isthar-Innana
AUTHOR (SHE): I who had to track the heartbeat in the slow
stubborn growth of oaks
REPLICA: in three sols of frankincense, through mountains of
myrrh

    Chechenit'sya—in the lean-tos of love, without roses.

it's not masochism, everything the protagonist says is true:
the cemetery of murdered daughters and their azure, azure
through which peacocks stroll; it enters me by the mouth and
your father yanks out my heart, I manage to get to a first lake
which is a first lake of eternal ice. "The main thing, ma'am, is
that you're saved." Later they force me to play a role in the opera;
your father throws all my underwear out the window, smashes
all my plates, glasses and the small funeral mask of Kleist and the
portrait of Hölderlin, the Aeneid and the Lucretius and the Virgil.
They make me swim in the realm of a thousand and one atolls of
silver. "Just keep talking underwater and the sharks will retreat and
with them your father, who is my father and once more wants to
make love to me." I hate you, hate your guts! I'll wear the azure
cloak, sidereal shawl of Tschaika Ahasvero, the moon's about to
rise.—This poem is a homage to Ingeborg Bachmann—Ingeborg
is one of the author's mothers who travelled to Klagenfurt in the
depressed Carinthia region after crossing the Dolomites, where she
was often in museums of taxidermy. The author has other literary
mothers too, like Sylvia Plath or Angela Carter, also sisters, blood-
sisters and illustrious predecessors—it's not a matter of looking for
influences for what she writes but of creating herself a genealogy;
and yes, it's true she used bits of legend but what she didn't know
was which ones were and weren't the little Princess of Kagran
(which in *Fascinio* was misprinted as Kageran) and her foreign
lover. More snow falls on us every minute. I'll wear your white
Siberian overcoat, the astral shawl of Tschaika Ahasvero. Later it
seemed that your father was not exactly our father; he wore a suit
in which he played with horsewhips, with rifles, with pistols for
firing into the nape, he puts on these suits in the deep of night. On
top of this, Cassandra couldn't have existed, never; no god ever had
such power. God is a representation, like the State
in nuptial lettering, I'll write

"on the lyric subject of poetic enunciation"

not—to be clear—as one or another of the persons of verbalization but a limit of language, empty, in any case a-representative or a-figurative and which then unfolds a process of truth in language, of fictionality, of opening toward the sensory. To deny language this capacity for construction is to deny it the process of truth that unblinkers words. It's by means of this quality of limit that the lyric "I" can adopt all formulae not just of Rhetoric but of every other literary genre. Definitely, the Poem subsumes the world into itself—we enunciate nothing new. From this comes its fictionality, its movement toward, for example, the land of oracles without ever being oracular or prophetic (oracles are impossible today); toward the land of Epic with no glad return to any native soil; toward the land of concepts without being tempted—horror of horrors!—by a system; toward the land of narratives without, naturally, ever succeeding in telling any story, in scientific or other discourses; toward the drama and autonomy of the different voices that compose it and, why not, toward the land of mass culture, which is to say that of literary sub-genres

> *We allege that this subject is a kind of eighth passenger of language, foreign to any type of nation but never outside the politically "human"*

> *Thus the need for the title of this dissertation: "Ophelia, Alien: Star-Voyager" and I am sure that my listeners will not fail to note the resemblance of this a-signified of language to certain aspects of the conceptualization of the "feminine" in our current civilization and literary system*

marginal notes in a transient's notebook: I want to write and write without ignoring my gender, for this gender is my difference, but I don't want the "eternal feminine" at the price of imprisonment—Margarida—nor with a dagger in my breast—Juliet—; I can't see myself as Beatrice amid celestial choirs, nor as Laura, Emma nor Anna Karenina, and even less or the same—why not?—as the lady of camellias; nor murdering my children, nor weaving the voice of enigma, nor destroying ships, nor provoking the final Holocaust in Troy; nor with Apollo spitting me out of his mouth to heaven so that I can never again be heard, I want to be heard

thank you very much

----

the sun will be spinning in my chest
a whole system of galaxies in my heart

I'll wear your shawl of white wood-lily, of martagon,
of wood lily

so tell me now . . . where's Kiel?
my journey

you already know what to do with the blood, it's not going to happen
that eternity be the prize at the price of Creon, which is to say, from
the male side of the lineage, or that you'll endlessly couch the body in
divinations that mean destruction for the city—a destruction that doesn't
even belong to you. Better to sit on the dark side, the side that doesn't
shine on the Solstice.

(for Arturo Casas)

this is a personal poem; keep your nose out of it

the incessant gleam, unalterable, of vegetation
swirl of lacquers
of tiles
in the breakdown of all Kantian categories
Havana is so beautiful!
for the psychic
mangrove
that vaporizes your spirit, right now, it hurts and you have to shut
your eyes it's so vehement and unreal: acid, perfume
of swings that convert and transfuse you, one with the cyclone,
the breeze.
In the fainting
For my edification

Galle! dearest: I'm the richest woman on the planet and
so astonished in the face of such plenitude that I can barely write
this letter. I have to tell you a story that's a bit crazy but I must tell
it as it's my only way to get in touch with you and send you my
affection.

I must start by telling you that Buenos Aires from the
sky is a huge quadrilateral of gigantic microchips, interminable
and long, lankily feminine as are all or nearly all the cities of your
hemisphere and I must speak of Dora too because the line of her
disappearance, at its zenith, traverses the nadir of your own tale;
in short, I see Dora as appearance or disappearance but never as
an inhumed body—I've spent a whole year trying to understand,
to analyze and find a way out of this disquiet that while not
painful does yes give me continual anxiety; in the plane when I
perceived Lucia's small body and her topaz stele, I knew or had
the intuition that Dora could never be interred like others because
eternity, the eternity of Dora Diamant, was a different eternity, so
I'd have to speed up the publication of her work so that my friend

could at last find her rest which is not a flowering from the earth or it is a flowering but from difference, from the perfume of ink and the manuscript's heart. Only when her work is published will I be able to accept her definitive appearance, appearance of her writings among us, her plurality embraced in the commonality of mortals and perhaps in something more we might call cosmos or radiant matter of the species. Dora's perpetuity, of which I'm somehow guarantor, not by designation but by feeling, has thus the significance of a debt, an entity newly in the realm of the visible, of the political, in the space of the nation and of the possible or impossible independence of the nation, of thought, definitely. This idea, idea of the perpetuity of Dora, is a gestation and a birth too, a torrent surging out of the remotest depths of stone, a bringing to light.

Never before have words appeared to me with such startling weight and a terror close to miracle, so I write down impossible words that must be nurtured so they won't become confused. It's up to me too to take responsibility for the immortality of Dora's being and, even more, for the resurrection of bodies because, Galle, I knew women capable of uniting all the genetic material of the species in their wombs and resuscitating from among the dead those we need back again, because of the incompleteness of their existence.

Thus I spotted the body of little Lucía as the Southern Cross, constellation I'd searched out night after night in the skies over Buenos Aires, she was there in my arms forged in diamonds, and in your womb Galle, as annunciation, as revelation of a sacred script and condensed in a rhomboid or coagulation of all the boreal dawns of history, impalpable history, unregistered but in the gender codes that are her sole possible inscription.

This idea of eternity that doesn't correspond to any prior or after-life, the idea of the reappearance of bodies came to me with shuddering force, like the force of a power, a power common to all women. All this, the chance to pay my debt to Dora and the certainty of a womb that exceeds the global placenta of the universe, agitated me so much that today I can hardly write this letter and let you know that for me it is impossible to forget our shared days and the opulence of our meeting, and the difficulties and risks that it all entailed.

Such was my journey, a return across the celestial routes that cradle us. Buenos Aires is just like this, a great illuminated cerebrum or the sacrilegious name of the womb of my mother or mother of all saints—it's America as far as I can say—

our stay coincided with the 25th anniversary of the bombing of the Presidential Palace in Santiago de Chile and I had no choice but to face my memories. Allende fell, murdered one month after the birth of my eldest daughter; this crime, and the memory of the brutal repression in Galicia carried out by the Falangist ranks of General Franco, destroyed in me forever any belief that democratic process was possible as a way out. The existence of powerful oligarchies allied with capital which in peripheral territories adopt untold forms of violence render any respect for a decision of the majority unbelievable. It stunned me, the dominion of these terrifying groups who control the state and military class to ensnare the majority of the nation, the majority of citizens and population, leaving any possible social articulation and all possible legitimacy for their culture outside the law. The cruelty of this situation stunned me, the practical non-existence of a social fabric, which reinforces ties of family and friendship as the only ones possible. So much stuns me! The zeal of capital, the avarice of its expression, that total illegality which reduces the population of the continent to a life of precarious invisibility, to a continual destruction of memory, and the entire population to an illicit condition of violence. It's not just that public health care and education networks don't exist, but that the state acts to guarantee that the nation is not possible. In such a way that the possibility of building one's own culture is stymied for the great majority. The sensation of moral fraud, of theft of their identity, is surely one of the major charges against the American oligarchy. Murderers alive and respected on both sides of the ocean, just as the Falangist murderers still live amongst us in Galicia, and their accomplices, those who shut up, who play their role, who acquiesce, who silence.

Novelty stuns me too, the capacity for change, the speed of learning, malleability, the throng; their use of language, a carnal language that caresses or slaps you but that you can always feel directly, without mediation, on skin, on flesh, on the intelligence of the emotions, the enormous capacity for desire, solidarity, the real youthfulness of their consciousness, their disinterestedness, the high level of technology, the impossibility of equality, difference and coexistence with this difference, religious freedom, and even emigration, Argentina's great *Centros galegos* held and tamed by every possible kind of clientelism; apart from the ever-steadfast Federation of Galician Organizations, you could say that most groups are generally despicable and rejected en masse by second-generation Galicians, which is to say by those born on the continent, the memory of expulsion, a certain rancour toward a land that dislodged their parents, together with real and present love, together with enormous curiosity about Galicia that is typical of the youngest who, as children, put up with the idiocy of all the folklore of Francoism

we visit Montevideo awhile to rest from the vertigo of Buenos Aires, the endless days of its inhabitants, the incessant rhythm of their lives; but also because of the stunning poems of Delmira Agustini and because it's the city of Isidore Ducasse, whom I so admire. Montevideo is futuristic and colonial, a city bursting with statues though the only female bust is that of Rosalía de Castro over in the Costaneira gazing at the implacable Rio Plata, a river I never understood because it's hard confronting the alien Nature of the south, even the jungle in the tropics is archaic, fossil, neogothic, and its rivers are cataracts that turn fainting into marble or nearly immobile waters, as if they didn't want to wake the vegetation on their banks from its dream. Thus the mouth of the Iguazú in Paraná, thus the nameless waterfall where I thought I'd found the white titan, the abyss of Arthur Gordon Pym, his embraces. At times a plantation of monkey-puzzle trees, a forest of cedars and cypresses reminds me of the writings of Otero Pedrayo, in the most northern and romantic of his novels,

.... I felt myself generally the product of a very ancient civilization, burst from a very ancient chrysalis, even older than Amazon jungle, I felt barbarous, European, as millenarian and precambrian as the indigenous gods, so alien to me, were basaltic. My ribs felt the weight of geodes, their igneous movement, marble waters. Eternity seemed quick, fulminant, velocious, energetic, inalterable, traversed by the hereditary dispersion of bodies: Obbatalá, I kept thinking

It's not my age or the distance between me and my memories that I recall but satiety in the face of language. At times my body takes the shape of an inverted ring and my ears register frequencies valid in every idiom. Perhaps
Buenos Aires was the city of love, of encounter, of embraces
city of Tschaika Ahasvero
and whoever possesses the face of the stars
the power of the orchid
of Atlantic honeysuckle
can open the letters of destiny.
God is but a living entity in the slavery of the flesh

> "We're all this if we come from afar."
> Cosmic Southern Cross in american sky
> sacred palaces and nights shone for us"
> *(Xohana Torres)*

—fragments of a letter sent to Graciela Leis Paris—:

Ada

(for Teresa López de Lerma)

> these days the entire cosmos is a linguistic sign—the human being, male or female, doesn't need to be in the centre, nor be the measure of the acts of god—today the universe is an infinite network of languages, thus the incommunicability of the poem

ANNOUNCER (SHE): Brenda, could you tell us when it was that you decided to give free rein to passion in your life?

BRENDA: it was caused by a dream; I was staying at the Hotel Beatriz in Teguise on Lanzarote, you know that island where five metres underground every tree root is a furious thicket; I was at a conference on inadequate beings and venomous snakes of the world, my room was a suite with mirrors, in the style of international tourism, the ambiance excited my libido and the conference left me exhausted, at the end of the day I slumped on the balcony and thought that this, really, was what my professional life as a zoologist offered me—contemplation of the night, of its serenity and of vegetation that simulated a desert, walkways between volcanoes, fish, hotsprings, the Atlantic so close to the Tropic of Cancer—then I had the first dream, over time I just recycled the information

ANNOUNCER: can you tell us that dream?

BRENDA: it was in a cellar (of my house) I think, and from the earth, surging from the depths and breaking through the floor, a priapus appeared, huge, powerful; it was the priapus of a king, of a faun, of some mythological figure and endowed with impetuous energy, it seemed a void and was drunk, naturally; I woke up in total anguish and had to masturbate right away

ANNOUNCER: but you were already subject to an earlier attraction to language-thought

BRENDA: I decided they weren't incompatible, that the trick was precisely to live both at once, especially the new one, the incessant lunacy of the scene. I had a second dream later

ANNOUNCER: similar to the first?

BRENDA: similar but different; you'll see: even as a child I was overly fond of games of chance, of circus and theatre and even of disguises

ANNOUNCER: tell us about your aunt's wedding dress

BRENDA: gorgeous! white satin, buttons covered in the same fabric, triangular plunging neckline, goddess

ANNOUNCER: in fact, one of your first 'actions' in collaboration
with María Ruído in the NaSA Hall in Compostela—

BRENDA: we didn't do it, I think we ran out of money, but we
did build a house of terror and paradise, in which the spectator
underwent various gymnastic exercises of contortion and balance,
and thus participated in a simulacrum of his own suicide

ANNOUNCER: Brenda, will you tell us your second dream?

BRENDA: we were in a fairground booth or amusement park,
totally surrounded by mercury, in a special compartment,
cylindrical and spinning, the throne mirrored too, a space capsule
of the old sputnik type; imagine a salon like Versailles and, in the
middle, our spinning double seat, we're belted in, lying down;
I was definitely tied to the king, supposedly we were playing
Hamlet or some other Shakespearean tragedy; it was an erotic
symbol, we spun at vertiginous speed, couldn't touch ourselves,
our field of vision was configured for a multiplicity of scenes, our
bodies twisted, circling and twisted again, masturbatory, hypnotic,
as in the case of symptoms of hysteria; it was the scene of an
impractical passion. During it all I was reading Apollonius of
Rhodes

ANNOUNCER: you've often declared that in our day the poem is
incommunicable; could you explain why?

BRENDA: the poem as conceived in modernity was based, as
everyone knows, on the centrality of metaphor and on free verse
and on free association of images as well; to insist today on its
communicability is chimærical, so much so that it's more effective
to occlude the poem and relate its context; every linguistic field
is already pure metaphoricity, so it's better that we let metaphors
emigrate and focus on production of the text, on its generative
system, in other words on the explicatory genesis of its semiotic
performance

ANNOUNCER: would you be so kind as to explain this again in more
detail for our listeners?

BRENDA: let's take an example: look at the classic line *the doves,
tremulous, fell upon her breast*, it's a beautiful verse of high sensual
content but perhaps it's more interesting to look at the moment
when a person reads it, relate what happens to this person,

describe the ambiance in the house, what the person feels, what perturbs him or her, what kind of determination arises in this reader, in sum, the issue is to narrate or generate a new type of poem where the agency of the line is what's critical and not the line itself, perhaps this is how we could attract the reader

ANNOUNCER: what would be more powerful then, the reader's decision or the line or poem she reads?

BRENDA: the protagonist's decision to give free rein to passion in her life starting from the verse of Apollonius of Rhodes, despite being subject to an earlier language-thought

ANNOUNCER: this new, incessant alteration of the scene

BRENDA: the instant when the doves really fall and the word is incarnated in her body

ANNOUNCER: will you build gallows? or use your hands?

BRENDA: now don't put executioner's gloves on me, nor the scarf round my neck, and don't stuff my windows with horsehide. Call me out but don't try to tame me

ANNOUNCER: Brenda, any vice you'd confess?

BRENDA: eating chocolate

ANNOUNCER: not confessable

BRENDA: zoophilia! (guffaws)

ANNOUNCER: and if you could reincarnate yourself?

BRENDA: as a caiman, for sure (laughter)

ANNOUNCER: your hobbies? what do you do in your spare time?

BRENDA: taxidermy, I'm wild about taxidermy museums, and water-skiing, which I did as a child in the summer on the Rías Baixas

ANNOUNCER: a recipe?

BRENDA: crab crêpes

ANNOUNCER: a brand of make-up?

BRENDA: "Les Ténèbres" by Dior . . . it's like savouring Gérard de Nerval bite by bite, I paint the Prince of Aquitaine's lips

ANNOUNCER: could you tell us about your most recent trip?

BRENDA: we toured the Colchis, that land as renowned and famed as it is unknown, my impressions were up on the web at: http:// www.corevia.com/teatrobruto, designed by Robert Bass

ANNOUNCER: let's go there now . . . screen!

I don't know if I ever went to the earth's edge and returned with a divine symbol, or not— really the whole tale of Jason is another account of origin, of legitimization of a lineage and its usurpation (such were my thoughts as I walked in autumn woods), when all's said and done what does the Argonauts' voyage mean?

I started with a poem by Paul Celan, it ends with the word *Colchis* and somehow includes the Anabasis; then I examined the mapa-mundi, the Black Sea, Caucasus, extreme limit of the ecumene; so this was Colchis, an inverted Geography that to Mandelshtam linked Russia to classical Mediterranean culture, to the Greek, to the slender white column or, even moreso, to a portico on the tundra and, by deduction, to the sea, to the Pontos Euxeinos, to the hospitable sea of ancient Ionia. Here he cradled his poems, in the Crimean peninsula where he'd unite Byzantine influence and Orthodox rite. For him, this was how the nation would establish itself in the face of the barbarity installed by the nights of Soviet black velvet; he'd confront this being—foreign to official and not so official culture—from the cornerstone of classicism held in the Western European tradition. For the poet Mandelshtam

as for the hero the journey to the horizon or finisterra was a quest for legitimization of his lineage in the face of usurpation, soviet in the first case and fratricidal and thus bloody in the second

For my part and going back to the start of this dissertation, I'll say that what I first noted was the man in sandals and the loss of the sandal (an attribute of civilization and of the road). The journey is aquatic of course; crossing a river and then, later, the communal tour through the pelagos, the unknown, the errant, the monstrous in Apollinius of Rhodes; the Colchi are characterized by the opposite of what we commonly call civilization; to give just one example I'll mention the burial of men in Colchis, we might conclude that death is the dominion of the wind, of sighs which rhythmically rock the male corpses hung in high boughs of the tamarinds, wrapped in oxhides. Matter impossible to consign to the earth's bowels, the masculine in its radical difference Medea

I don't know if I ever heard the prow of a ship speak nor if I ever saw the many eyes of Hera, scanning the shining surface of the waters. I don't know either if I ever had a flask with the elixir of mortal love, nor if I battled fire-breathing bulls, nor if I sowed the furrow with dragon's teeth golden, the fleece today enfolds the hero entirely, or someone else,

purple mantle, sign and alliance
with the isle of murdered
women who are my own
premonition. I'll ask forgiveness
clumsily from Circe for the
betrayal of that most perfect
and divine of lineages, the
wild lineage of the ocean (but
everyone already knows what
happens to princesses among
the Hellenes, in the end they
marry a god and live happily in
the constellated empires)
I recall oh with clarity the city
walls, the mandrake rooted in
the gallows and a philtre, yes
poisonous too, for forgetting.
The chant, immortal chant
of my treason, song that lulls
the serpent lulls the frozen
mornings of fear
It's about islands, islands
that populate the sea. Argos,
constellation of the south, ship.
All origin, all tales of origin are
an ideological construct. A debate
around who legally controls the
city. Then spiders, mermaids
from here to the Anabasis, arrival
of the 10,000 in retreat from
the land of the Colchis. Here's
where I arrive at my own truth:
crossing rivers, trekking across
plains, the fantastical animals
and the flatlands: Salamina,
Amoroce, the Limia—the golden
fleece symbolizes the womb; life
emanates from here, it's where I
was, in those entrails, in the fleece;
I can recognize my beginnings, in
the wool, in the sheep, my own
embryo growing in wool, in golden
fleece—Chaldean—. The power to
engender now covers the full height
of the hero

ANNOUNCER: when you speak of a post-apocalyptic subject, what
are you referring to?
BRENDA: a subject is an entity that formally exists in a time, and
I refer here to the notion of a time marked by the Apocalypse,
in other words, a time or narratology that starts with the six
days of creation and ends in the second Parousia or judgement
or tribunal of God. A subject like the one I propose is, clearly,
not one that occurs after the A., but one who negates this very
conception of time and thus rejects the catastrophe; it has to
be noted that, although the decentralization of God and even
his death were long ago announced by Philosophy, capital or
huge transnational corporations still propagate this sort of
belief, in everything from growing militarism to the languages
of medicine; my conception of the subject is a different way of
again confronting this kind of deployment
ANNOUNCER: the concept of a new type of subject that

84

destabilizes the prior univocal-cultured-renaissance subject and its later fragmentation or dissolution, is fundamental for you, Brenda. Could you give us more detail?

BRENDA: it's not just a new type of subject we have to talk about, but a new assemblage of diverse types of enunciation that cohabit in discourse and are thus not one but multiple. In our own case we could speak of at least three types of historical subject: a pre-organicist agrarian one linked to our particular way of idealizing ancient agrarian communities, this is a pre-modern or pre-renaissance communitarian subject, a Homeric subject; secondly, we've the Cyclopean-masculine subject of modernity, Mallarmean; and now this new subject, post-catastrophe

ANNOUNCER: when you say "among us," are you referring to a specific ethnicity?

BRENDA: ethnicity these days substitutes for the people, in its romantic sense; it's an essentialist and static position that's never interested me. Better to talk of nation, of the subject that deploys this notion with the political will to be or constitute a nation, as thought, sovereignty, decision and action. What defines us as different is our own particular conception of origin and its narratologies which directly confront the narration that constitutes the monolithic state, a state resolved to overlook the illegality of the former regime and which admits neither plurality nor difference; because of this, we have to go on narrating origin and trying to legalize it, to remember it over and over again. On the other hand, the three subjects of whom we just spoke and who constitute us also mark the possibility of independence, as much in the desire to move toward that political will as in its thwarting or in the impossibility of us moving between discourses so different and even contradictory. This consciousness, this capacity to live with and endure this incessant balancing act, is a mark of our courage and thus the decisiveness of our difference

ANNOUNCER: in your recent talks you reject the notion of gender

BRENDA: the notion of gender stems from the culture / nature dichotomy and was used quite effectively by archeological

feminism to oppose sex-nature/gender-culture. These
essentialist types of constructions are no longer operative. Quite
simply, biological differences don't exist
ANNOUNCER: what differences exist between representation and
simulation?
BRENDA: as you'll see, representation means substituting an
original with a copy; these textual procedures centre on the
desires of a monodirectional subject or cyclops eye that expressly
manipulates its readers from a privileged position; in simulation,
there's no substitution, rather a situation is created, ludic or not,
in which the contracting parties agree to exculpate themselves
from the obligatory effectiveness of the very contract, or thing
forged by imagination. We're talking here of a principle of
inclusion not of exclusion from the orb, or orbit,
if you'll allow me
ANNOUNCER: if you weren't who you are, who would you want
to be?
BRENDA: in a kind of oceanic way, "manifesto of jellyfish,"
perhaps through the oceans
ANNOUNCER: Brenda, can you describe the genitals of your text?
what is your next project or desire?
BRENDA: Titanic, the credits for *Titanic*, they're impressive, it
would be to write like that, with that structure, something epic,
an epic, in homeric columns, which is to say: hexameters

this book m-Talá
is for Iris Cochón (there weren't so many
problems earlier)

to the REDES ESCARLATA

interrupt the reader. So

YOU'RE INTERRUPTED

METAPHOR: in a sense predating the modern LYRIC revolution
(substituting finally, a "degraded" language with another
supposedly UNIVERSAL)

body—metaphor—linked to an earlier AGRARIAN MODE OF
PRODUCTION, which requires annulment of all difference
in its poetic PROPOSITIONS

METAPHOR is fields of GRAIN
THE SNATCHING OF PERSEPHONE
THE DESCENT INTO HELL
THE RAPE
MATRICIDE

METAPHOR: monarchy

this ASIATIC-FEUDAL-SEIGNORIAL-BANKING
mode of production is used, as it decays, to slow the advance of
new productive forces
>in LANGUAGE—to reverse—language's centrality
>its emancipatory power

>that takes the place of production
>that impedes all production—free, at last, of the
inclemencies of CLIMACTIC change, unfavourable

>metaphoricity: TRANSPORT
>LYRICAL
>removed from any act of mimetic fabulation
>any duty of Representation (the method by
>which the subject/poet relates to the poem's
>subject, identifies with it or dissimulates behind it:
>*lexis*)
>any hierarchy

in that place where no-one writes

>and these aren't organicist, pseudo-Universal forms—as in
Homer
>>nor evanescent symbolic forms (retrograde)
>>"not an experience of self or discovery
>>of nature or sensibility, but A NEW
>>POLITICAL EXPERIENCE OF THE
>>SENSORY or A SENSORY EXPERIENCE OF
>>THE POLITICAL"

PLAGUE METAPHOR MONARCHY
>the body of the king that promises harvests, whatever the
mode of production—today
>>the supposed autonomy of his canons
>>his sanctity (in the a-political idea of art):

>BOURBONICAL

a toast to Stéphane M.

NOT ONLY DID WE SKIP THAT MANOEUVRE
      GULPED DRUNK INTO THE CHIMÆRA'S JAWS

not a chance
      A FISH THAT CAN SIDESLIP THE ABYSS

not URSA-constellation and the SHACK
      the little theatre on the outskirts where the animal
reaches erect-human position the trainer is then a TREE OF LIFE
      stick close to me
            I'M NOT AN OBJECT OF THE GAZE

EVERYONE IN ICEBERGS
      like MERLIN

—ooh, prince
the forest is the sigh of my soul
kiss sire these my pale lips, pale as death

      JUST LIKE MARTIANS

SO IT'S a tomb
                    the most beautiful of birds

          unforgettable swan

          TEARDROP
BLACK PLUMAGE   SPACE
                    DAWN

the reader's inside the POEM
the multitude

—hey humans!
don't run away, we're your friends

                    BE IT
               with garlands of paper icicles
     where oil and phosphorus burn HYPODERMIC-GIGANTIC

               NOT SPUME
               THE FISH THAT SIDESLIPS THE ABYSS

so there's
CRACKS
CRACKS IN THE ABYSS

VENTRAL: we had gunpowder

        exocet-black-hole and the star

suddenly
  sucked into FOG

     bitter prince
              virtual
              of the void

the cracks are OURS
    our leonine body

the multitude's in the poem
the concept

          along with your calyxes and herbariums and
          your celestial maps and the ballerina
          ILLITERATE FLOWER

       DON'T DANCE
            write

and the Mermaid
little cartesian Mermaid, imaginative abstract
she who separates

        nothing: on the fabulous Hallstatt collections
        on the exquisite statuette of Willendorf
        of the adorable collection of skulls

she knew, yes, she knew
it was you: she loved you. All my poems were like this

IMPOSSIBLE
INCONCLUSIVE

        you were in the flow of waters. Speaking of abandoned
machines. As if I were strapped in, as if I couldn't have
withstood it. I don't know when we saw the sea and night, the
last of my nights, of all my nights. Light dawned SMITING US,
that light that burst from dawn, raw, OCHRE, smote us

  TRANSCRIBE
      THIS GIRL EMPRESS WARRIOR HELMET
                  IN THE FOLIO OF THE SKIES

EMPRESS-LITERATE CELESTIAL-WARRIOR HELMET-
CELESTIAL-EMPRESS

CRIMSON

SPUME

—don't think, don't start thinking now about what
happened to the FAIRY, after such hibernation

but all these vases
                    like cottonwood reeds
            —so that you suffer

it's possible
it's possible it had its start here
when I saw my father's genitals, just like that, naked

            but I'm still a girl
            right at the height of the Father's genitals, of the husband's

            little

I'm starting to see Literature as a construct of the intellect. I try
to think of it that way. To use its phrases

BURST FORTH HEART!!!

IMAGINATIVE ABSTRACT

n.: TOAST

and bleed.

                                        (June 19, 1997)
                              Thurs.

She-Hrg hires an assassin:
a Hymen for the baptist

but this is my language too

I can share this language

huh?,—wazzup, what's happening?

                    She-Hrg wants to kiss the sun, so
the author he sets the table and dusk falls:

sun dances in her hair and we all get the picture, I think.

                    but She, I never saw Her, never
here, I never saw her anywhere, it's the first time.

The grotto opens to the outside
a frigid outside—this image I remember, remember forever
because of what I saw, what I saw in this place   in the beginning
                  this is what I saw, she—other—she
            right in this crevice, enchained

  The sky so blue, so cold, a dusk that she—other—she couldn't see

she—other—the only one in chains.

                  She-Hrg strolls, wanders to and fro and
there are lions, the lions are the same
as those of Maria Aegyptica: the same lions
but a different story.

Maria Aegyptica is not around here
not right now she's not;
I won't tell the story of Mary of Egypt right now.
But the lions, yes
are the same and adore her feet.
                        the Author he writes that her feet can halt the sea.
The lions are desert lions—solstice in the desert—Maybe there's
another dungeon, maybe it's not the same as the one opens to the
dusk, the one where she—other: she couldn't see
Maybe the women were never together
maybe I never laid eyes on them.
She-Hrg stands, very quiet, very erect, a desolate figure: YET
ANOTHER DESOLATE FIGURE. The Author he says her hair
is like the lion's mane, that lions live in an enamoured skull, that
CALYXES fall from her clothes

                                    yet this doesn't take place here
but in the pond, where She, She-Hrg, does something with the lilies
and the lions pull calyxes from her clothes
        the lions have to pace around her
it's a HOT dungeon
hot if we compare it to the desolation of her face
it's a cylindrical burrow, a deep den, open to the skies
a TUNNEL OR WELL CONSTRUCTED WATERLESS
Hrg meets the feral ones there
the feral ones are there only for Her, to be with Her
the feral ones live in a circus, underground, in a dune

                    Later everything CHANGES

She wants to kiss the sun
the worst of all kisses. The Author sets the table, metal plates
She dances
there's always a guest, a mysterious guest, veiled face, and heavy
curtains, with various and many layers, very dense,
and furniture with chimæras and at some point someone cracks the
secret of this furniture

—autumn: night—
sepulchre of my dreams
funereal and darkness descends the slope
on horseback
the Author, the Author no, he takes the stairs and there's an opal
and a tremendous racket in the sepulchres
—you really don't know how to tell a story, do you
mother-of-pearl: Heraldic

to explode and inundate a goldsmithy   infinite CHANCE

            the author's voice
celestial

affirms, does what She-Hrg utters
regarding the metals, Earth's telluric forces. She hires an assassin,
has a purse of linen, this purse; hey, it could be remnants of a
pure race of her ancestors, remnants like
infinite and chance, vertigo and madness, remnants like
                                                ABSOLUTE
always the same stranger, veiled and layers of fabric, the Author
likes fabric, ornate cloth, fabrics. He sees it all as a drama. As a
SHIPWRECK—to see it as he does—spiderweb in the
fold of a veil. The Author he must speak, utters verses
—*if the idea of death were not already dead*
death. So She hires an assassin. The Child sings some silliness
about feelings and tenebrae and his vertebrae. I can't feel any
sympathy at all for the Baptist. Before, I didn't feel any for the
author either. And there's a swan, swans, we all know, are poets
Later too, in the Shipwreck
                                    the assassin kills John
which makes Her pensive

finally he explains She grew up, that someone raped someone

                                    an Alexandrine verse

the old poetry now: HYMEN
the new poetry
                    hires an assassin

        he who rules the rudder of my existence guides forth my ship

—O dagger!   here rust and let me die
                              falls on the body: dies

            if I bluff
            when it's my
            turn and throw a 12,

                              it has nothing to do with chance

tis a poker of PURITY

Mother

the book bound in gold that holds a golden legend

        may you dream of Mab
        of the carriage of the queen

—and the icebergs?

—you can put them in the fair-booth on a floor of mirrors

                in the zoos
                in the Zoologicals

$\longrightarrow$

next to the Romanian buffalo

HESPERIDES

NOTES ON THE TEXT

Galicia (Galiza) is an "autonomous community" (not as autonomous as a Canadian province, not as autonomous as Scotland) in the NW of Spain, with its own language and culture for over 1,300 years. Galician, which is older than Castilian Spanish and survived centuries of Spanish colonisation and decades of oppression under Franco's dictatorship in the 20th century, thrives tenuously, but thrives. It is the root language of modern Portuguese, but is a separate language, as Portuguese orthography and pronunciation developed differently after Portugal's independence.

Rosalía de Castro (1837–1885): 19th century poet of the Galician renaissance who wrote in Galician as well as Spanish, in an era when other writers did not use Galician for it was considered uncouth. "Galicians, never call yourselves Spanish." A literary and folk heroine in Galicia ever since, though today her use of regionalist and Galician images and language is at times vaunted more for folkloric reasons than for revolutionary ones. As Margarita Ledo says, Rosalía is a kind of episteme in Galicia.

Xosé Luís Méndez Ferrín (1938–): poet and novelist who started publishing during the Franco régime, mostly in Argentina and Switzerland, and who spent time in jail for agitating for Galician freedom. A signal figure whose presence marks the 20th century of Galician poetry and fiction irrevocably; every writer writing now in Galician is in his debt. If Mendez Ferrín had chosen to write in the colonial language, Spanish, we'd all know his work. But he chose to live fully in his own language, in a state, Spain, where the central government (unlike Canada's, for example) does nothing to support languages of the so-called "peripheral nationalities."

Ramón Otero Pedrayo (1888–1976): Patriarch of Galician Letters, Conscience of Galicia. A singular and monumental figure in the cultural and political history of 20th century Galicia. Teacher, essayist, novelist, member of *Xeración Nós* (Our Generation),

Galician nationalist; he stood all his life for the cause of Galician identity and for a Spanish republic, in the form of a federation—which would give Galicia more autonomy. He taught Geography and History at a college in Ourense and, after a hiatus of 14 years (removed from his post at the start of the Civil War, he refused to grovel to get it back), at the University in Santiago de Compostela. From 1950 to his death in 1976, he headed the publisher Galaxia, a major force in nurturing culture and language during the long night of Francoism, and still a major publisher today.

Lois Pereiro (1958–1996): poet, contemporary of Chus Pato, sorely missed figure.

Manuel Outeiriño (1962–): poet and translator, contemporary of Chus Pato.

Praza da Quintana: famed open square of beautiful Galician stone in Santiago de Compostela in the old quarter. Walking across it is indeed a good idea. You can see it at http://www.crtvg.es/camweb/index.asp?id=11&mn=COR

Xohana Torres (1931–): poet and older contemporary of Méndez Ferrín.

NOTE ON THE COVER

The Latin background text is drawn from the treaty of friendship signed in 132 A.D. between the Coelerni (a Celtic people who lived in the author's native area of the Limia) and the invading Romans. The image is a photograph of the Code of Hammurabi, copyright © John Said, 2007.

*9 7 8 1 8 4 8 6 1 0 4 5 3 *